# Live and Be Counted

## A Novel Inspired by True Events

*Dedicated to my grandfather, to my great aunt and to all the Holocaust survivors who lived to share their stories of survival and found the strength to teach us the traditions of our past generations*

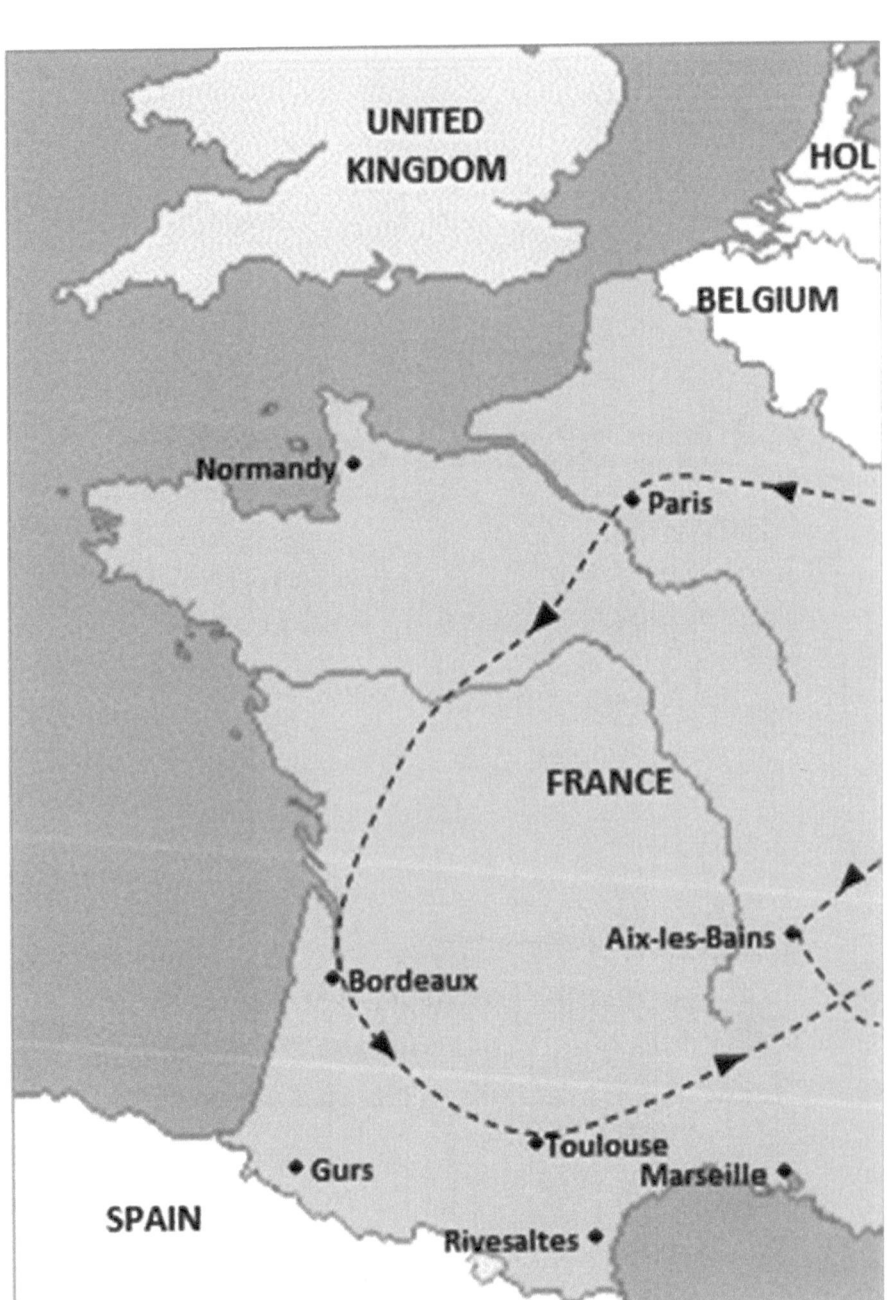

Copyright © 2021 by Ronald Siesser

All rights reserved. In accordance with the U.S. Copyright Act of 1976, the scanning, uploading and electronic sharing of any part of this book without permission of the author constitute unlawful piracy and theft of the author's intellectual property. If you would like to use material from the book (other than for review purposes), prior written permission must be obtained by contacting the author at ronald.siesser@gmail.com. Thank you for support of the author's rights.

First paperback edition, October 2021

The author is not responsible for websites (or their content) that are not owned by the author.

ISBN 978-1-716-38828-6

Acknowledgement is made to United States Holocaust Memorial Museum for permission to print images appearing on pages 245 and 246.

10 9 8 7 6 5 4 3 2 1

**Printed in the United States of America**

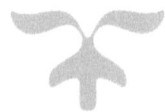

*"May Reuven live and may his people be counted in the number."*
*(Deuteronomy 33:6)*

Moses' End of Life Blessing
to the Tribe of Reuven in the Sinai Desert,
Prior to the Israelites Entering the Land of Israel

# Introduction

April 1, 2020

"Papa, you're on mute! You have to click the microphone in the bottom left corner of your screen so I can hear your voice."

Eli sighed as he watched the facial features of his great grandfather magnify when Papa brought his iPad closer to find the microphone icon. Features that Eli felt Papa sported quite well, considering his ninety-three years of age. Eli's school project required him to interview his great grandfather, and he was beginning to worry whether the conversation would ever take place.

"No Papa, now you turned off your video. You need to turn your video back on and click the microphone button so I can see and hear you at the same time!"

To his family, he was called Papa for three generations. To everyone else, he was Alfons Sperber, the steadfast man in the neighborhood, still with a full head of hair, who loved technology. He was, after all, a retired electronics and appliance salesman with a voracious appetite for the newest innovations that came to market.

Alfons would, no doubt, learn how to use Zoom.

It was three weeks since a global pandemic had been declared. COVID-19 was mercilessly sweeping around the world and already had claimed thousands lives. As doctors and infectious disease experts scrambled to find treatments, hospitals became overwhelmed by the volume of patients who presented with

## Introduction

severe breathing difficulties and high fevers. Healthcare workers, trying to treat those already infected, were themselves contracting the highly contagious virus.

Governments around the world wrestled with a mounting public health crisis and ordered everyone to stay home as the most practical way of slowing the spread of the virus. By the middle of March, restaurants, retail stores, public parks, workplaces, houses of worship and schools were all shuttered. Millions of people saw their livelihoods vanish and unemployment rates spiked, toppling even the worst year of the Great Depression in 1929.

Eli himself, a precocious pianist with an insatiable thirst for learning, was also dealing with the realities of his world where schools transformed to Zoom classrooms, educators became quaran-teachers and birthdays were being celebrated virtually. Parents who had spent considerable effort trying to tame their children's addictions from digital screens before the pandemic surrendered to the realization that online school was the only antidote to keeping their children meaningfully engaged during the day. For many parents, new ways of virtual working meant focusing on their jobs while their children simultaneously went to school from adjacent rooms at home.

Eli usually spoke to Papa cursory every other week, asking how he was feeling and exchanging their highlights. The conversations were predictable and lasted no more than a few minutes. For his project, Eli needed more attention from his great grandfather and Papa's fidgeting with Zoom was making him increasingly skeptical.

At the point of despair where Eli was about to give up his interview, Alfons' video and audio came together that relieved the tension pulsating through in his ten-year old frame. "Papa, I can see and hear you now. Just make sure you have enough battery

**Live and Be Counted**

life in your iPad so it doesn't die!" Eli forewarned, anticipating another setback.

Alfons leaned his iPad on the dining room table using the kickstand and his warm face came comfortably back into focus. Eli smiled at the familiar sound of his great grandfather's voice and could almost feel the soft-shaven skin of Papa's cheeks from their hugs after in-person visits.

"Papa," he started. "I have an immigration project I'm doing for school. I need you to tell me how you came to America."

# Part One

## Vienna, Austria

# Chapter 1

September 1937

Alfons darted down the steps of the cathedral-like Akademisches Gymnasium after his first day of school of sixth grade. Situated in the Innere Stadt district of Vienna's city center, the Gymnasium was known as one of the most elite and demanding schools in Austria, with its focus on humanities and languages, preparing its students for advanced academic studies.

Alfons' work ethic in his elementary years at Stern Yeshiva earned him strong enough grades to gain him admission to the Gymnasium. Leaving the Stern Yeshiva, which provided a dual-based curriculum in Judaic and secular studies, was not an easy decision. It came at the cost of Alfons needing to part from the familiarity and comfort of his Jewish friends he had largely known since his birth in 1927.

The leather satchel, secured by the strap across his shoulder, swung back and forth from the weight of his new books. He was ten years old, halfway toward turning eleven, and it would be the first time he would tend to customers from behind the cash register of his parent's raincoat and sports clothing store.

It was early September and summer temperatures had just started to give way to the fall chill, which meant townsfolk would be shopping for winter coats, rain jackets and ski suits for the cold seasons upon them. The store had a continuous flow of customers nine months a year, except between June and August when it was difficult to imagine bundling up against the warm breezes rushing through the Austrian countryside and humidity taking over the city streets in Vienna.

His mother, Elsa, ran the storefront in Salzgries shopping district just a few blocks from the banks of the Danube River in Vienna. With his father, Alexander, overseeing the manufacturing, Alfons was expected to report to duty after school to help around the store. For several years, Alfons was excited to part of the small business operation, tasked with unpacking and inspecting new apparel in the stock room for unraveled seams and broken zippers. Eagerly, he swayed his parents to promote him to the front of the store where he would be more visible and interact with shoppers.

Elsa was in the early stages of a pregnancy and was expecting a new baby in May. Alfons' parents, who were both forty-one years old at the time, were going to need his help in the store one way or another after the baby was born. The timing of the baby's arrival was fortuitous since the late spring and summer months were spent planning and producing for the next set of seasons, and there was less foot traffic in the store. Alfons could certainly handle customers, under the moderately watchful eyes of his parents of course, while he was in summer recess.

The global economic depression was still unforgiving in most parts of Europe in 1936 and 1937, even as recovery was taking shape in other places. Germany and Austria infamously led most of the developed economies in unemployment, with nearly one out of every five able-bodied men unable to find work. The depression took away jobs but did not keep the cold weather from knocking, and their coat and ski suit business was doing relatively well despite the despair misery around them.

During the prior winter, the Sperbers made auspicious use of the ski suits from the store and vacationed in the Altenmartk ski area, about a four-hour drive to central Austria in their new Buick Century coupe. Alfons and his parents enjoyed skiing the

## Chapter 1

mountain trails by day and reading by the fireplace in their lodge at night.

Alfons recalled how proud his father was the day in December 1936 he brought home their first car and announced that they would be going on a winter vacation to a ski lodge at the end of the month. It was shiny and black import from America with two spare tire encasements just setback above the front wheels. Alfons was equally excited that his parents permitted him to bring a friend on their trip.

His family kept a kosher home, which meant separate meals for dairy and meat, and separate sets of dishes on which they were served. How they observed kosher at home was exactly the way in which he was taught to keep kosher in school at the Stern Yeshiva. Kosher animals which chewed their cud and had split hooves needed to be prepared in a ritual way by the local butcher, and certain animals like swine were biblically prohibited.

For *Shabbat*, Elsa made a chicken soup that tasted the same each Friday night, and that was a good thing since he would not have wanted it any other way. The carrots and dill melted in his mouth along with the chewy *pupiks*, or chicken gizzards, she threw in. She also made a large *cholent* with white potatoes, pearled barley, kidney beans, and shoulder cuts from cow beef that could serve more than a dozen people.

Often it did.

Their *Shabbat* table regularly hosted his aunts and uncles and their children for festive meals and joyous laughter following prayer services at the synagogue. His father led melodious singing around the table from the selection of songs found in the *Shabbat* section of the prayer book. Between seven sets of aunts and uncles spanning both his parents' siblings, Alfons had more first cousins than he could count on his two hands, including cousins that lived right across the street from their apartment in Vienna.

As the business was growing, Alexander was increasing his travel from Vienna to all different parts of Europe to buy raw materials and, in turn, export finished coats and sportswear that came off his manufacturing lines. Initially, Alexander relied on business contacts he had created in the 1920s while working for an accounting firm in the apparel industry before he decided to try his own entrepreneurial adventure. Those contacts opened doors to other capitalists that became a tight network of suppliers and buyers across Europe, forming the backbone of his apparel business.

Alfons understood the importance of his father's travel, and while he would count the days until his father's return home, he never bemoaned his father's time away. Instead, he looked forward to his time at home being regaled by the sweet, classical sounds of Bach, Beethoven and Chopin that his father played on their Bechstein upright piano, the centerpiece of the Sperber's living room.

Alexander found delightful enjoyment playing piano and was known in the Viennese musical circles to tune cacophonic keys so that children who were learning to play could hear the musical tones in the right way. Sometimes, men from the synagogue joined him in the apartment where they played and sang Jewish and classical melodies together for hours.

Toward the end of the summer just before classes at the Gymnasium were scheduled to start, Alfons had his first taste of Paris. For fifteen hours aboard the *Express d'Orient*, which originally connected Paris all the way to Istanbul when the railroad first opened in 1883, Alfons accompanied his father on a trip from Vienna to the fashion capital of Europe. In Paris, they spent nearly a week taking in the emerging styles, meeting with designers and

## Chapter 1

negotiating contracts to supply raincoats and sportswear with retail stores up and down the Champs-Élysées.

With each store they entered on the heavily trafficked Paris promenade, Alfons followed his father proudly as he determinedly closed on sale orders that would be ready for the upcoming autumn. Alfons had never seen this side of his father's business, just the viewpoint from the storefront helping shoppers peruse their selections and hoping – sometimes persisting – that a browse would turn into a sale.

On the last night of their seven-day trip, they were joined by a few men at a small café in the Jewish Quarter. Sitting outside in the warm breeze, the square was still teeming with restaurant patrons and the sun seemed to hang in as long as it could, reluctant to fully set into the west. Alfons did not recognize the men that joined them, and they did not seem to pay much attention to the young boy. He listened intently as they talked about rain jackets, winter coats, ski suits, import taxes and predictions of optimistic snowfall that would hopefully drive sales.

One of the broad-shouldered, balding men spoke about the wind tunnels created by the skyscrapers in New York City that made winter temperature feel twenty degrees lower than what the mercury measured. He wore a tweed sports jacket with an open neck shirt and moved his cigarette in and out of his mouth in between sips of wine. Alfons picked up that his name was William, a distinguished name he felt for a successful American businessman.

"You know Alfons," William turned to him and smiled. "I remember when you were a baby. You were a big boy when you were only a few months old. My how you have grown! How old are you now?"

### Live and Be Counted

Alfons felt proud that one of his father's partners was taking an interest in him amidst the adult gab and shop talk. "I'm ten and will turn eleven next March," he answered dutifully.

"Well young man, your job is to keep growing," William instructed with a warm smile, as if it were a choice truly up to Alfons. "I have a feeling that you'll be destined for great things."

The group continued their meal, shared some laughs and toasted to cold and rainy temperatures, climates that would unquestionably stimulate sales. As they were finishing the chocolate eclairs for dessert and their third cups of French wine, the conversation turned to politics.

"Tell me, Alexander," William the man from New York inquired, "how are the Jews of Vienna feeling about Hitler's rise to power in Germany?"

It was the first time Alfons had ever heard the name Adolf Hitler.

## Chapter 2

April 1, 2020

"An immigration project, you say?" Papa repeated Eli's request back to make sure he had heard him correctly. "I think I can help you. Let me ask you first, what do you know about the Holocaust?" Papa asked gingerly, unsure how much his ten-year-old great grandson knew about the events in Europe eighty years earlier.

"The Holocaust?" Eli asked, curious how it related to Papa's immigration to the America. "I know that the Holocaust happened a long time ago and a man named Hitler was responsible for killing six million Jews." As he spoke, Eli started to feel derailed that Papa wasn't telling him what he needed to complete his school project.

"To tell you how I came to America, you need to understand why I was forced to leave my home in Vienna, Austria. Adolf Hitler was the reason we had to flee," Papa prefaced.

"Papa, is this going to be a long story?" Eli asked impatiently. "My project is due next week, and I also need to ask you for the recipe of a favorite food you used to eat."

"For many years, we rarely spoke about the events during the Holocaust. It was a chapter of our life that was closed." Alfons sometimes talked about the people who helped him hide, but never shared the full extent his experiences. The memories were simply too painful to talk about. Yet, each year there were fewer and fewer Holocaust survivors that remained alive, and he wanted his stories passed on to future generations.

### Live and Be Counted

Eli was becoming fretful about finishing his project on time, but he was also recognizing the importance of the moment. He straightened up in his chair and readjusted his face into the center of the Zoom screen as Papa began. He had heard that there were Holocaust survivors still alive today, but it never occurred to him that his great grandfather was one of them.

"Life started to become difficult for the Jews around 1933, when I was around six years old. Germany was still feeling the humiliation of losing World War One fifteen years before. As part of the peace treaty that ended the war, Germany was forced to pay other countries money to help rebuild their cities after the damage and destruction it had caused. These payments were called reparations."

"OK, so Germany lost World War One and had to pay," Eli repeated trying to keep up. "What happened in 1933 that life became harder?"

"In 1933, Adolf Hitler was elected Chancellor of Germany, which was second in command. When the German President Paul von Hindenburg died the next year, Hitler became President and promised to restore Germany's prosperity."

"What did those promises have to do with Hitler's hatred against the Jews?" Eli asked, trying to make the connection. Stories from the Holocaust were told occasionally at school and at home, but he never heard about the political events that led to the anti-Semitism and genocide of European Jews.

"In the 1930s, Germany's economy was suffering and had widespread unemployment. When people are desperate, they will believe anything that gives them hope," Papa reflected. "Hitler blamed the Jews for Germany's despair and made people believe that prosperity would return if the Jews were marginalized from society."

## Chapter 2

"Why did he blame Jews? What did they do?" Eli asked disturbingly.

"A lot of Hitler's hatred for Jews brewed while growing up in Austria," Papa related. "Some people have said that Hitler blamed a Jewish doctor for not being able to cure his mother's cancer which was too far along to respond to treatment."

"Wait!" Eli interjected. "Hitler was born in Austria? How did he become the German President? Wouldn't he have to have been born in Germany?"

Alfons appreciated the connection his great grandson was drawing to his familiarity with the laws of the United States where someone could not be elected President if they were born outside of the country.

"Before the borders were drawn that you see today, the German Empire was a group of loosely organized cities with ever shifting territories and alliances. Austria literally means the 'eastern' side of the German Empire. Austria never developed a unique language. Even today, Austrians speak German and take on many of the German traditions and culture. So being born in Austria was not a hindrance toward becoming Germany's leader."

He continued, "Growing up in Austria, Hitler's views were shaped by the hatred he had for minority groups like Jews, Czechs and Slavs who had different traditions. He developed an especially deep hatred for the Jews because he saw them prosper, while he was barely making ends meet."

"Hitler himself was an aspiring artist who was rejected from Vienna's Academy of Fine Arts, not once but twice. He was told that his personal works were considered amateurish, but some historians have said that Hitler blamed his rejection from the Academy on a Jewish member of the admissions committee. He spent the next few years trying to peddle oil paintings to tourists and shopkeepers in Vienna, while his hatred of Jews and other minority groups escalated."

Eli wondered if history would have been different if Hitler had become an artist.

"Vienna, Austria was becoming increasingly diverse, which Hitler detested," Papa continued. "He moved to Germany to serve in its army at the start of World War One, where he would be surrounded by others who shared his German identity. He was awarded medals for bravery and his popularity rose after the war, speaking about the superiority of the German race and wanting to reunite Austria with their original German roots."

Alfons turned to his left where Phyllis, his wife of the last twenty-five years, came into the room carrying a mug. Alfons' first wife Clare of nearly forty years succumbed to lung cancer in her early sixties and he found companionship with his neighbor Phyllis Black, who lost her husband to heart disease a few years after Clare died. They kept each other healthy, sharp and entertained.

"Thank you Phyllis," Papa leaned in to give her a kiss on the cheek.

Eli could see steam rising from an odd-shaped mug, which seemed to have a semi-circle opening rather than full cylinder at the top. He strained his eyes to get a better look at the words across the mug, which he deciphered as 'You Asked for Half a Cup of Coffee' and shrieked at the sense of humor coming from his great grandparents.

"Papa, what we were just talking about?" Eli traced back the last few thoughts from their conversation. "Hitler. Germany. Bad economy. Blaming the Jews."

Alfons explained that Hitler's promise to restore German pride grew popularly amongst Germans, leading to a swell of

## Chapter 2

support for his National Sozialistische Workers Party that controlled all aspects of the government and military.

Eli now understood where the word Nazi came from.

"This was an awful turn of events," Papa reflected. "Hitler used his stage to incite hatred toward the Jews and began to strip them of their civil rights, leading to unprovoked assaults, vandalized synagogues and desecrated cemeteries."

They continued to talk about how life in Germany began to change with Hitler's rise to power. Papa admitted that the anti-Jewish changes unfolding in Germany went largely unnoticed to him living in Austria where he was enjoying a relatively normal childhood by going to school, playing with friends and taking family vacations.

As Eli shutdown his iPad to get ready for dinner, he began to think if anti-Semitism and Jewish hatred could rise similarly in America nowadays as it had in Germany in the 1930s.

## Chapter 3

February 1938

Alfons was slowly finding his stride at the Gymnasium in his first year. He enjoyed Mathematics and Language Arts, honing his skills in both French and English, but making new friends wasn't easy in sixth grade. He missed the familiarity of the children that continued at the Stern Yeshiva reading Hebrew, learning the stories of the Bible and hearing about key figures in Jewish History. It's not that Alfons felt ostracized in his new school, he just felt different. He looked forward to seeing his old friends who attended the synagogue to which he and his father walked from their apartment for *Shabbat* services each week.

There was one other boy who accompanied him from Stern Yeshiva to the Gymnasium. Ludwig Manheim lived around the corner from Alfons and the two had known each other for as long as their young memories would allow. Ludwig's family identified strongly with Jewish culture, but they did not observe all the same traditions that the Sperbers did. Ludwig was attracted to the intricate rituals, which is why he enjoyed spending *Shabbat* with the Sperber family.

Alfons and Ludwig often spent afternoons riding their bicycles, skipping rocks on the banks of the Danube or playing checkers in the yard. They built snowmen on wintery days and cooled down in the sprinklers on hot summer ones. When Alexander offered to take one of Alfons' friends on the ski trip the prior winter, Alfons immediately selected Ludwig with whom to brave the snowy slopes.

## Chapter 3

When Alfons turned eleven years old that March, Ludwig gifted to him a book. It had a hard, green-colored cover with three-hundred and ten pages. The book was written in English and Alfons knew exactly Ludwig's motives to practice their English in real-time and improve their fluency. They were learning English at the Gymnasium and even at this early age, recognized the importance of mastering it to be successful in the developed world. Ludwig had the same copy for himself and they sometimes convened a book club consisting of the two of them.

Alfons and Ludwig came to their teacher Herr Gerhart's classroom several times a week during the recess period decoding additional math problems beyond what was given to the rest of the class. Neither of the boys minded missing the free time outdoors. To some extent, recess math was an escape from unstructured, free play that sometimes left them excluded from dodgeball and football games.

Herr Gerhart sensed an inherent insecurity among the Jewish boys and watched how they grew strength from each other's companionship. Anti-Jewish sentiment was growing in neighboring Germany and there was growing indications that their classmates were not accepting them into their groups. As the bell rung signaling the end of recess, Alfons and Ludwig were besieged solving for 'x' in an unusual polygon. Alfons suggested that Ludwig come to his parents' store after school where they could finish the problem.

Later that afternoon, Ludwig greeted Alfons' mother, who was behind the counter. Elsa was amused that her son was almost a head taller than Ludwig, but the boys did not let that get in the way of their friendship. Soon, Ludwig became a regular in the store after school, helping Alfons inspect the new coats and hang them on the racks. They sometimes spread their books and homework pages across the shop floor after all the coats had been hung and giggled about the classmates who had gotten into trouble in Herr Gerhart's class for talking when he turned to the chalk board.

One afternoon, Ludwig keenly observed that Alfons would soon no longer be the only child in his family.

"When is your baby due, Frau Sperber?" he blushingly asked Alfons' mother one afternoon.

Elsa smiled as she placed both hands over her belly that gestured the baby was growing mightily strong inside. She regarded the high cheekbones and dimples that Ludwig sported along with his blue eyes and envisioned a handsome young man was in the making.

"Oh, just a few more months, Ludwig," she said. "The baby is scheduled to arrive in May, with God's help. Alfons will have to spend more time in the store for a few months while the baby is young until it's old enough to be left with a nanny. And since Alfons' father has been traveling so much lately, I'm going to rely on his help at home too."

Ludwig was more than slightly overwhelmed on behalf of his friend by the idea of having to go to school, help run the coat store and manage chores around the home. "Alfons is one of the most dependable kids I know. I'm sure he'll make you and the new baby proud."

"He always does," Elsa replied. "Ludwig, please join us for dinner the next time you come to the store."

And Ludwig came, more than once.

# Chapter 4

April 5, 2020

Eli sent Papa an email after one of his morning virtual classes. "Papa, can we continue talking at 3:30 today after school? You still haven't told me about your journey to America," he wrote. At the bottom of his note, Eli pasted a link to a Zoom meeting that Papa could join. Eli was starting to feel the anxiety inexorably creep from within his stomach, worried that we would not be able to finish his immigration project by its due date. When the time arrived, Eli opened the meeting and could hear Papa through the computer but was unable to see him. He struggled with futility trying to explain again to Papa how to start his video and soon just relented.

"Papa, let's continue without video today. I can still hear you and we need to get to the point where you come to America. Before you start, there's a question that's been bothering me since we last spoke."

"What's been bothering you, Eli?"

"I feel like this is a bizarre question to ask," Eli crept. "How did people know to call it World War One if there wasn't yet a World War Two?"

Alfons laughed at the thoughtfulness behind Eli's question. "Actually, you're right. The world war that was fought from 1914-1918 was originally called The Great War. In 1939, when Germany invaded Poland and alliances began to form between England, France and the United States, it became clear that a second world war could develop. At that point, politicians, generals and journalists began referring to them as World War One and World War Two."

"That makes a lot of sense," Eli said satisfied with the answer. "Now, let's get back to your story how you came here."

Papa continued, "OK, but we still need to go back to March 1938 when Germany invaded Austria. That's when everything began to change. You see, Hitler viewed his home country Austria as a part of the German culture and had dreams about annexing Austria to help re-establish the great German Empire. Actually, some Austrians welcomed the *Anschluss*."

"They welcomed what?" Eli stopped Papa before he could continue with the next word. "I think the Zoom connection got bad for a moment."

"The *Anschluss*," Papa repeated. "The unification of all German-speaking people under one flag. Since the break-up of the Austro-Hungarian Empire after World War One, very few people believed that the tiny country of Austria could survive on its own and there had been talks about joining Germany ever since. This idea dated back to the end of the Roman Empire in 1806. Teachers taught about *Anschluss* in a favorable light, so the idea of unification was embraced by many Austrians."

"Austrians who identified with the Nazi party and supported the *Anschluss* conspired to seize the government by force and unite the nation with Germany. Austrian Chancellor Kurt von Schuschnigg, learning of the conspiracy, met with Adolf Hitler in the hopes of reasserting his country's independence. Instead, Hitler demanded that von Schuschnigg appoint members of Austria's Nazi party to the government or face an invasion by the German army."

Papa continued, "Fearful that Hitler intended to take over Austria, von Schuschnigg called for a national vote to take place so

# Chapter 4

that Austrians could decide for themselves whether they wished their nation to remain independent or become part of the German Empire. When Hitler heard this news, he decided to invade Austria immediately to prevent the vote from taking place. Schuschnigg gave into pressure from Hitler and resigned in March 1938 pleading with Austrian forces not to resist a German advance into the country."

"The next day, Hitler accompanied German troops into Austria, crossing over the Saalach River that separated the two countries and declaring *Anschluss* in the city of Salzberg just over the border. There was no resistance, and Austrian crowds that culturally identified most with Germany met the soldiers with enthusiasm. The German army continued 300 kilometers east to Vienna, Austria's economic and political capital, where Hitler put von Schuschnigg in jail. From that point on, Austria existed as a federal state of Germany."

Eli contemplated if taking over Austria was as easy as rolling a seven or higher in the game of Risk. He allowed a faint smile to form across his face, thinking about the 'The Game of World Domination' that he sometimes played with his friends, tucking the unfinished board game underneath the couch, and pulling it out the next week until one of the boys controlled the world and was declared winner.

"Before the Holocaust, Jews played an important role in Austria's economic and cultural life. In 1938, Austria had a Jewish population that was approximately two-hundred and fifty thousand people. Jews made up almost four percent of the total Austrian population and nearly nine percent of the census in the Vienna capital, which was an important center of Jewish culture and education."

"Hitler was bent on destroying that?" Eli kept pace with the history he was learning.

## Live and Be Counted

"Originally, the Nazis made life in Vienna very hard for us," Papa confirmed. "They wanted to drive us out of Austria and, as Jews were gradually robbed of their civil rights, some fled to neighboring countries. Jews were blocked from going to their jobs, Jewish students were shut out of schools and universities and we were prevented from attending synagogue."

"Papa, isn't that what's happening now? The government has basically ordered my parents not to go to work, has closed down our schools and is preventing us from going to synagogue."

"The coronavirus is a public health enemy that is disrupting everyone's routines," Papa said. "The lockdowns imposed by the government is being done to protect your safety, not to intimidate or drive you from your home. Still, you're experiencing something in your lifetime that I experienced when I was the same age, which is being held back from freedoms and activities you've had your entire life."

"How was life different for you after the Nazis took over Austria?" Eli asked.

"Initially there was no physical harm, but the Nazis made it clear that they were in control. Just a few days after they arrived in Vienna, there was a city-wide parade where all the Austrian's came out to salute Adolf Hitler. The Nazis made this into a celebration so that Austrians, especially those who were less sure or resistant to Germany's vision of reunification, would welcome their arrival. The Gymnasium postponed classes so that children and teachers would come out to the *Anschluss* parade in support. It was hard for us as Jews to know how to feel because there was so much unknown," Papa lamented.

"Ludwig came to my apartment that morning since the view from my balcony of the parade route was far better than his. We were young, ten years going on eleven, so while there was

## Chapter 4

anxiety and apprehension from my parents, there was curiosity and novelty with me and Ludwig. At one point, when my parent's attention was diverted to something else, we slipped out of the apartment and down the steps to the street to be with the crowds. The only thing I remember from that day was the sky opening with rain while we were in the streets. It was still blustery cold in March and we left our coats behind with the impetuous decision to escape from the apartment. I thought for sure we were going to get sick being out there."

Alfons paused and reflected to himself that perhaps the rain was God's tears foreshadowing what was to come.

While he was collecting his own thoughts, Eli was already navigating the Internet. "I just did a search on YouTube," he said excitedly. "There is actual video of the parade. It's black and white, but it looks real."

Alfons couldn't recall if video cameras had been invented yet. He surmised they must have been around.

"I'm going to share my screen with you and we can watch together," Eli informed him, about to pull off a Zoom miracle in his great grandfather's eyes.

In a moment, Alfons' iPad screen flickered from Eli's round face and auburn curls to a black and white soundless movie streaming a cavalry of tanks, horses and soldiers crossing a river. He immediately recognized it as the Saalach River separating Germany and Austria on the western border. About two minutes into the video, the images changed from the countryside to the city of Vienna with apartments, townhouses and storefronts. In addition to the tanks, horses and soldiers, there were also dozens of black vehicles carrying men in uniforms.

On both sides of the street, hundreds of people, adults and children alike, stood in coats waving flags. Some groups of children, Eli reasoned, were classes from school who were brought to the parade to welcome the Germans. He remembered Papa telling him that many Austrians liked the idea of being unified with Germany. He also considered the possibility that the students were simply told by their teachers to cheer and salute the Germans in the parade with their outstretched hands.

Eli's initial excitement of discovery of the video rapidly turned to fright seeing red Nazi flags being waived by soldiers from one of the vehicles. He recognized the black geometric symbol in a white circle, which looked to him like four rotating arms coming from the center. He knew the Nazi symbol was linked to racism, fear and death. He saw more and more flags moving through the screen as the vehicles passed.

"That symbol on the flag," Papa explained to him, "that is the Nazi swastika."

Suddenly, Eli's heart beat harder than he ever felt before, a swell of panic rushed across every inch of his body. His eyes locked in on a uniformed man sitting on the top of the backseat in a shiny, black roofless car waving his hands to the saluting crowds, first on his left side and then on his right side.

The man's short-cropped black mustache was unmistakable.

"That's Hit… That's Hitler, isn't it?" Eli stuttered, stunned by who he was seeing. "Papa, is that Adolf Hitler?" he asked just to be sure.

"Yes," Papa answered with despair audibly in his voice. "That's Adolf Hitler."

"Papa, were you at the parade? Do you think you can find yourself in the video?"

## Chapter 4

Alfons had wondered that himself. He and Ludwig had snuck out of the apartment to sit on the street curb where the parade was going by, but at eleven years old, neither of them could forecast or understand how bad it was going to get.

"A few days before the parade," Papa recalled, "Nazi soldiers accosted Father as he pulled up to our building in his Buick Century coupe and demanded the keys so it could carry soldiers in the parade. Father resisted the seizure and tried to rationalize that the vehicle was insured only to him. The Nazis scoffed at him, lifting their rifles and pressing the tips against his chest, and said that the Fuhrer would gladly pay for damages the Buick suffered."

"The Nazis just took Grandpa Alexander's car?" Eli reiterated in disbelief. He was beginning to understand the impermeable power the Nazis were exercising.

Alfons knew that his father wasn't naïve about the hatred that Hitler had for the Jews, but even as a young boy, he did not imagine their property being confiscated. "Father had no choice and turned over the keys. We never saw the car again," Papa answered.

Alfons refocused his story how the environment in school began to change. Eli corrected his posture in the computer chair, not wanting to miss what he was about to say.

"During the first week after the *Anschluss*, I didn't notice anything different. A few days after the parade, children in my school came dressed in new uniforms that looked as if they were in the military. These were uniforms of the Hitler Youth, *Hitlerjugend* as it was called in German. Throughout the day, they saluted the red Nazi flag. Ludwig and I started feeling uneasy, unwanted at the Gymnaisum. Herr Gerhart actually pulled us aside during one of our recesses in and told us it wouldn't be safe for us to attend school anymore. My parents were beginning to feel the same way and did not send me back after the second week."

"What happened to Ludwig?" Eli could see Papa lift a finger to wipe away a runaway tear from his eye.

"It wasn't that big of a deal that I hadn't seen him for a few days since my parents decided to have me stay home. They hoped the atmosphere at the Gymnasium would calm down and it would be more comfortable to go back to school. On *Shabbat* afternoon, I walked to Ludwig's apartment and knocked on his door for several minutes, but no one answered. I started to feel nervous. Then, from the corner of my eye, I saw some movement from an elderly man wearing a yarmulke emerge from his apartment down the hallway. I recognized him from the synagogue, but never spoke with him."

"What did he say?" Eli was hanging on with suspense.

"The elderly man told me that he saw the Manheim's leaving their apartment carrying suitcases the night before. There was a lot of commotion. A baby was screaming, the mother was shouting, the father was instructing the older children to move along without a word."

Eli could sense Papa's voice trembling through the computer's audio. "I ran all the way home, suddenly fearful of my own surroundings, suspicious of everyone around me. I kept wondering why the Manheim's would leave their apartment so suddenly at night, and without even a goodbye from Ludwig."

"Papa, what happened to them?" Eli asked, fretfully.

"I don't know if the Manheim's fled the country or if the Nazis arrested them and sent them to the concentration camps." Papa choked up a bit and brought his hand to his mouth. Eli could

## Chapter 4

see it was shaking slightly. "I never saw Ludwig again," he said desolately, his voice cracking.

Eli asked himself why the Jews did not protest or resist the Nazis actions. He was seeing on TV people gathering in parks and on marching on streets with signs demanding the government to release the pandemic lockdowns. He was still considering the parallels of the two time periods.

"As weeks went on, some Jews who tried to contest the Nazis were beaten or arrested," Papa paused for a moment to collect fragments from his memory that hadn't been evoked since his childhood. He considered that maybe the Manheim's were arrested because Ludwig's father did not surrender his car to the Nazis for the parade.

"One day in April, about a month after the *Anschluss*, my father and I were closing the store to go home for dinner. Three or four German soldiers marched in and casually browsed through the coats, trying some on. When they began to leave the store still wearing the raincoats, Father pushed me down below the sales counter, hoping to keep me out of sight, and tried to confront them."

Alfons could still hear the sinister cackling from the soldiers when they kicked his father to the ground.

"They humiliated him, making Father scrub one of the officer's shoes with a toothbrush while the other solider thrusted his boot into his chest. I watched the Nazis pull Father up by his collar and throw him into the street, brutalizing him while cleaned dirty spots on the pavements outside the store with the toothbrush."

"Papa, it must have been horrible to watch them beat your father. Were you hurt, too?"

### Live and Be Counted

"The Nazis didn't see me initially, but when I saw them handcuff Father's hands behind his back, I sprang up from behind the counter and helplessly begged them to let him go. Father cried back at me as they dragged him away. *'I'll be alright'* he howled. *'Tell Mother I'll be alright.'*"

Alfons stopped suddenly. The intense pain he felt many years before witnessing his father's arrest made it difficult for him to tell the story over to Eli. He took a few deep breaths and Eli could see the agitation in the expression on his face.

At the same time, Eli was stunned. Papa's story was becoming personal and harrowing. First the Manheim's' disappearance, now Grandpa Alexander's arrest.

"It's OK, Papa. You don't have to continue if it's too hard," Eli reassured him.

"Thank you, Eli, but I want to. It's important that you know what happened." Papa straightened himself up in his chair, cleared his throat and brought forward the courage to continue.

"The burden I had telling Mother what happened to Father was unbearable. She was so distraught and questioned if they would ever see Father again. She was hearing about Jewish men being arrested and sent to the Dachau concentration camp in Southern Germany."

Eli interrupted, having heard distantly about concentration camps on Holocaust Remembrance Day in school. "Aren't concentration camps where the Nazis brought Jews to be killed in gas chambers?"

"In the final years of the Holocaust, gas chambers and crematoria were installed in the concentration camps across Germany and Poland to mass exterminate Jews. In 1938, these camps were overseen by German soldiers to manufacture weapons and other supplies using forced labor made up of Jewish men and women who were being held as political prisoners. Dachau was among one of the largest labor camps."

Remembering the first anguished night at home after Father's arrest, Alfons and Mother recited chapters of Psalms together, which was a traditional ritual many Jews had when crying out to God for help. Alfons pleaded with God that Father return to be there for the baby's birth since his Mother was nine months pregnant. His aunts and uncles came to the apartment with hot food and snacks, keeping them occupied with conversation, but there was little solace.

"Suddenly after three days, we were speechless when Father opened the door and stumbled into our apartment. Mother threw her arms around Father, and I wrapped my arms around both of them. Father tried to hide the bruising from the beatings he received, but the discoloration under both of his eyes were especially visible."

Eli reacted, "Why did the Nazis release him? Didn't you say that Jewish men were being sent to the Dachau labor camp?"

Alfons was coming up for a break. Recounting memories of his childhood after more than eighty years was harder than he initially imagined. "How about we pick up the rest of the story tomorrow?"

"You got it, Papa!" Eli reacted enthusiastically. He hadn't expected to be drawn into Papa's story when they first started. "I'm sending you a Zoom link right now."

# Chapter 5

May 1938

The Hotel Metropole, which was in the city center of Vienna along the Danube River, had been transformed by Germany into the Nazi headquarters soon after the *Anschluss*. Franz Huber, a German solider, commanded a staff of nine-hundred officers, eighty percent of whom were recruited from the Austrian police. The hotel became the central operating center of the Nazis in Austria and where they brought Jews to be interrogated, tortured or deported to concentration camps.

Franz Huber was appointed Vienna's chief of the *Geheime Staatspolizei*, or Gestapo as it was abbreviated, which operated as secret police that gathered intelligence about Jews and acted to arrest any dissidents who resisted their rule. The Gestapo officers arrested Alexander outside his own store, bringing him to the Hotel Metropole and throwing him into one of the guest rooms that had been turned into a holding cell.

Alexander remained in the room for two days, subsisting on just a few cups of water and a bread roll that the Gestapo mercifully gave him. The Gestapo gave no indication what they were going to do with him, he feared that he would be rounded up with other arrested Jews and send to Dachau. He thought and thought until he conceived a plan that he hoped would enable his release. Toward the end of the third day, Gestapo officers entered the room and handcuffed his hands behind his back.

"Wait!" Alexander pleaded. "I have an idea that will help the Germans. I have access to foreign trade and currencies that

## Chapter 5

the Germans need if they're going to supply their soldiers in Vienna. Please, take me to Franz Huber, let me explain my idea." Less than a month after the Nazis established control over the city, all the Jewish residents knew the notorious name Franz Huber as the one in charge.

The Gestapo officers looked at each other, not knowing what to do. They agreed to inform Huber and let him decide if he would see to Herr Sperber.

"*Heil Hitler*," the officers announced as they entered the doorway of Huber's improvised office off the main lobby, saluting the commander. He extended his right arm from his neck into the air with a straightened hand. There were three other Gestapos sitting around the desk.

"*Sieg Heil*," Huber returned in kind, signaling his obedience to Hitler and the Nazi party, but he was more annoyed at the interruption by the officers at that moment. "This better be important. We are working on our status reports for the Fuhrer now that he has returned to Berlin."

"A Jew is being held in room 317 and is asking to speak with you directly. He's a local businessman and if offering us something we may need. We arrested him the day before yesterday in his store on Salzgries."

Huber placed his hands on the desk, pushed back the chair and stood up straight. He wrapped his dark green military jacket from the back of the door across his shoulders and slipped his arms through the sleeves, flattening the red badge of the Nazi symbol sewn onto the left arm. He patted his holster for a weapon and grinned. "This better be good, Lieutenant."

Alexander was sitting on a chair in the hotel room, his hands handcuffed behind his back. He had dried blood crusting around his nose and mouth, and purplish-blue bruising was visibly showing around his orbits and cheekbones. Huber looked pathetically up and down at him and reasoned his height was probably no taller than five and a half feet tall. He wondered what idea could possibly be that innovative and important to pull him into an interrogation room.

"Herr Huber," Alexander addressed him with respect that was probably more driven by fear but did not show through his boldness. "Thank you for seeing me. I believe that I can help you."

Huber made mental note of his poise. "I'm told you are Alexander Sperber, a shopkeeper in Vienna who harassed my soldiers while they were purchasing items from your store." Huber tapped his foot impatiently on the floor.

Alexander knew that the truth had been twisted to tell a fallacious story, but it would have been futile to try and contest the facts as Huber relayed them.

"Herr Huber, I own a raincoat and sportswear business with partners all over Europe. In six months, your men will need proper attire to keep them dry from the rain and warm from the cold. Let me go and I will re-purpose the output for your soldiers' benefit. Simply give me a fair price for my production so that I can buy fabrics, buttons and other materials and continue to pay my seamstresses."

Huber mused at the notion that a local supplier could get him garments needed for his men more efficiently than the supply coming from the labor camps in Germany. He also knew that imports from other countries like England, Holland and France would dry up as the war progressed and interrupt supply chains. Yet, he wasn't convinced that he needed Alexander's help.

Alexander saw the doubt in Huber's eyes and put forward another argument. "I will increase production not only to supply your soldiers in Vienna, but to continue my sales across Europe.

This way, we will bring hard currencies into Austria, which is needed to maintain the economy during war. British pounds, French francs, Dutch guilders," he listed.

At the sound of hard currencies, Huber paused momentarily and considered the idea. Motivated by his worth to the Fuhrer, he could potentially look like a genius back in Berlin if he could reliably supply wardrobe necessities to his units in Austria. He also knew it was important to keep people working as the war progressed and bringing cash into the country would help. One business would not carry the entire economy, but with increased production he could put additional Austrians who were unemployed on the sewing tables.

Huber agreed. "I expect weekly reports on your output. My men will arrive on Fridays to pick up the finished goods and manage the distribution of the coats and outerwear with the officers."

Even if it meant he was supporting the German war effort, Alexander reasoned that keeping his family alive was worth the exchange. A few hours later, Huber gave him papers that certified his business was now under his auspices, stamped with the statement that read *'For the Good of the Economy of the Third Reich and the Fuhrer,'* permitting Alexander to carry out his business operations free from harassment of the Gestapo.

On the next morning of his third day in captivity, Alexander Sperber was released by the Nazis, hungry and weakened, already refining a plan that he hoped would enable him to escape the Nazi grip and move his family to safety.

## Chapter 6

April 8, 2020

When they resumed their Zoom session a few days later, Alfons recounted his father's experiences under Nazi arrest. "Wow," Eli marveled at the cleverness of his great-great grandfather. "Your father was very lucky. He made the Nazis realize that he was more beneficial to them managing his business than being in a prison or labor camp. I guess things haven't changed all that much compared with today."

"What do you mean by that?" Papa asked quizzically.

"Well, the Nazis essentially told Grandpa Alexander what he needed to produce and for whom. Isn't that like the US government requiring car companies to make ventilators instead of vehicles?" As he spoke, Eli doubted himself whether the comparison he was trying to make was logical.

Alfons wasn't in agreement but appreciated Eli's figurative thinking. It took many years after the Holocaust for survivors to truly uncover the extent of the Nazi atrocities and the role of the US in liberating Europe from war. Much of the United States' victory in World War Two was attributed to the way the country unified behind the soldiers who were sent overseas.

"After I came to this country, I learned that President Roosevelt had ordered the Detroit automakers to put all their resources into tanks, military trucks, jeeps and other equipment needed for World War Two. In wartime, the President has the authority to order companies to produce things on an emergency

## Chapter 6

basis and distribute critically needed supplies before other buyers on behalf of the government."

"What do you think President Roosevelt would have done if the companies refused? Could he have put its business leaders in jail?" Eli was still trying to rationalize if the two scenarios were more the same than they were different.

"That's a good question, but the situations were different. During World War Two, the US government gave financial incentives, tax breaks and loans for companies to shift their production on the government's behalf. Most Americans were unified in the fight to liberate Europe and business leaders, many of whom probably had family members or friends enlisted in the army, did not want to create a bad reputation for their companies by refusing to help."

Alfons was hearing on the news that not only were car manufactures making ventilators, but apparel companies were making facial masks and beer companies were using excess alcohol to produce hand sanitizers. "Today, the US President is invoking the same powers to fight coronavirus as President Roosevelt did during World War Two," he relayed. "Besides, the government isn't intending to control these businesses forever. Surely, they will turn decision-making back to company leaders as soon as we get control of the health crisis."

"What happened after Grandpa Alexander came back home?" Eli asked.

"Following Father's release from his arrest, he increased production and began sending shipments of coats to the Germans. It turns out, during our trip to Paris the summer before, Father had opened a bank account and established a small satellite in the 9th district, sensing that the climate was worsening in Vienna and that we might need to leave. Father wrote letters to his buyers across

## Live and Be Counted

Europe asking them to send payments to the new address on Rue Lafayette. This way, we would have money waiting for us in Paris."

"Over the summer," Papa continued, "treatment of the Jews in Vienna worsened and many fled if they could. Unprovoked street violence against Jews escalated and some were even shot for slight infractions, like looking in the wrong direction when a Nazi officer demanded attention. Father knew we would have to leave Austria."

"Many Jews indeed left Vienna, replanting in Hungary and Czechoslovakia, which neighbored Austria on the east. Some Jews who believed in the biblical promise of a homeland, joined small waves of *Aliyah* to chart a new trajectory in the ancient land of Israel to create a Jewish state free from persecution."

Eli was familiar about stories he learned from school about the establishment of the State of Israel in 1948. He detected there was a connection between the Holocaust and Israel, but he wasn't quite sure how. Maybe for another time, he said to himself.

"Something else happened soon after Father was released and returned home," Papa said with suspense. "My sister Helgi was born. I remember how proud I was to hold her. Father loved photography and used his camera to take pictures of me and Helgi after she was born."

Eli wondered how difficult it must have been having a new baby while the Nazis were occupying Austria. "How did you manage to escape from Austria to come to the US?" Eli cautiously felt optimistic that he was coming closer to being able to finish his project.

Papa continued, "Needing to create some order around a chaotic demand for exit visas, the Germans established the Central Agency for Jewish Emigration in August 1938 to accelerate forced

## Chapter 6

exile of Austrian Jews. The Agency was run by the Germans and created exit permits for Jews to leave Austria."

Papa paused for a moment. "Do you know who Adolf Eichmann is?" he asked Eli.

"Another Adolf?" Eli questioned, concluding that anyone with that name must have been bad.

"Adolf Eichmann was one of Hitler's right-hand men," Papa decided to keep Eichmann's background simple. This was already a lot to take in for a ten-year old child. "Eichmann was sent from Germany to become the head of the Central Agency for Jewish Emigration in Vienna. There, he appointed Josef Lowenherz from the Jewish community to be liaison with Jewish families that wished to leave the country, helping them understand the emigration process and completing their applications."

Alfons reflected momentarily back to happier times of his childhood. Josef Lowenherz had a cantorial voice and used to lead the services at his synagogue during the High Holidays. He sometimes sang with Father around their piano in the apartment.

"Jews who were permitted to leave Austria were imposed a hefty emigration tax. Since Lowenherz knew most of the families in Vienna, Eichmann used him to validate the personal wealth they were declaring for the tax. Lowenherz was obliged to flag for Eichmann any Jewish families seeking exit visas who were hiding or understating their assets."

"The Nazis used Jewish leaders against their own people?" Eli asked incredulously.

"The Nazis were in control," Papa replied, "but they needed intelligence from Jewish leaders who knew the ins and outs of the community. For many Jews who were able to leave, paying a tax was preferred than paying with their life. Almost

## Live and Be Counted

130,000 Jews left Austria over the next two years. However, as the Holocaust intensified, the Nazis turned the Central Agency for Jewish Emigration into a center for mass deportation in 1941 where most of the remaining Jews in Vienna were rounded up and sent to the concentration camps in Germany and Poland."

Eli was trying to visualize thousands of people leaving their homes, speculating if the total number of Jews who lived in his city would come close to reaching the amount that left Vienna. He also wondered how these families resettled in new places since they didn't have the Internet to plan for all this in advance.

"Secretly, Father was making plans," Papa resumed. "One night, I was awakened by Helgi's crying and overheard Mother talking with Father in the bedroom as she soothed the baby back to sleep. I crawled from my room and pressed my ear to their door, grasping onto each word. I heard them talk about leaving Vienna and going to Paris where being Jewish would not be a threat, where I could go to school without fear or intimidation."

"One of Father's buyers, probably someone I met during our trip to Paris the prior summer, owned a store on the Champs-Élysées that had an empty apartment above the retail space used for storage. It wasn't much, but it had running water and heat. He assured Father that if we ever came to Paris, we could live there, until we found something more permanent."

"Wasn't Grandpa Alexander protected because he was producing coats for the Nazis?" Eli objected. "Why would you have to leave?"

"I'm not sure Father would have called it 'protected,'" Papa differed. "He had essentially turned over control of his business to the Nazis under threat of deportation or death. Father knew that the Nazis could revoke their deal without notice or explanation. As soon as Father offered this arrangement to Huber, he knew he

## Chapter 6

would need to devise an escape plan. The Nazis would eventually take full control of the business and regard Father as expendable."

"It doesn't seem likely our government in the US would do that today," Eli concluded that government control of businesses during the pandemic had very different intentions and outcomes of Nazi control.

Papa continued, "In July 1938, Father went back to Paris to secure raw materials and other supplies needed to produce garments and raincoats for off-duty German soldiers. At least that's what he told Huber. Huber believed him since the French government was already restricting trade with Germany after the German army seized the Rhineland in 1936, a strategic waterway and industrial area on France's eastern border with Germany. Father would need raw materials, and so Huber gave him documents allowing him to travel through Germany into Paris and back to Austria."

Alfons recalled the strict instructions Father gave him to watch after Mother and Helgi while he was away. Alfons did not fully understand at the time that Father was secretly replanting his business in Paris using the space on Rue Lafayette. The raw materials that he was purchasing would be used to restart production in France, not sent back to Austria. He already had the space, and furnished it with cutting boards, sewing machines, assembly tables, storage bins and hanging lines. Payments from his buyers were already arriving to the new Paris address since the summer of 1937.

"Weeks into the precarious arrangement with Huber, Father was experiencing increased scrutiny from the Gestapo, demanding to see invoices and receipts. While he was in Paris, one of the Gestapo officers assigned to oversee the store intercepted a letter, discovering a bank cheque from one of Father's buyers with a note that read, '*I misplaced the Paris address and therefore sending money I owe you to Vienna. I hope this finds you well.*'"

"The officer, eager about his discovery, brought the letter to Huber who was meeting with Eichmann at the Emigration Agency. Concluding that Father had been deceiving him, Huber immediately demanded Mother's and my arrest."

"How did you know this had happened if your father was in Paris?" Eli asked curiously.

"Remember I told you about Josef Lowenherz, the Jewish community leader who was appointed to help process the emigration quotas?" Papa was connecting the storylines. "Lowenherz was with Huber and Eichmann when the Gestapo officer brought the letter he had intercepted. Lowenherz overheard the entire conversation and, being close friends with Father, secretly created exit documents for us after their meeting ended."

Papa continued, "I didn't spend a lot of time telling you about all my aunts and uncles who lived nearby in Vienna. There was one uncle, Father's brother, who lived in the building across the street from us. Lowenherz brought the exit permits he had created to my uncle and insisted they be delivered to us as soon as possible. If Lowenherz came straight to our apartment, he may have been suspected of acting criminally behind Eichmann's back."

Alfons cautiously approached a defining moment in his family's ability to stay one step ahead of the Nazis. It was September 1938, five months after the *Anschluss* since Germany occupied Austria and the unyielding grip of the Nazis was getting stronger.

"When my uncle knocked on our door and handed us the exit permits from Lowenherz, Mother knew we needed to leave immediately. We did not have the luxury of time to wait for Father

## Chapter 6

to come back from Paris to retrieve us. Mother kneeled down to me, holding Helgi gently in her arms, ran her trembling fingers through my hair and told me to pack a bag."

Eli felt his heartbeat racing with anticipation. "What happened next, Papa?" hoping he would finally hear about his journey to America.

Alfons did not reveal to Eli how difficult it was to conjure memories that were locked away so o long ago in his head. Even after he came to America, the years from his childhood were never discussed. There was a collective embarrassment, a humiliation of sorts over what had happened. Fellow survivors who found themselves in the United States on the safe side of life after the Holocaust rarely acknowledged or spoke about the dehumanizing treatment they experienced.

"Let's pick this up tomorrow, Eli. Grandma Phyllis is calling me for dinner. I smell tuna casserole, my favorite." Papa smiled and bid goodnight to Eli as he leaned forward to press the off button on his iPad.

Alfons replayed sorrowful memories from his youth that had been suppressed long ago. Leaving Vienna was one of the most difficult things he had to do. He didn't want to weigh Eli with the burden of such tragic experiences, but he also knew time would soon run out to tell his story.

## Chapter 7

September 1938

The night that Alfons' uncle delivered the exit papers from Lowenherz, Elsa and Alfons spent the next several hours packing whatever they could into three leather suitcases. Elsa calculated that each of them would wear a backpack and Alfons would carry two of the suitcases, while she carried one suitcase and baby Helgi in her arms. She was afraid that bringing a baby carriage would slow them down and not fit in the aisles of the train anyway.

Elsa packed a minimal amount of clothing. Her husband was re-establishing himself in the apparel business and surely clothing could be replaced in Paris. She was more intent on bringing valuables like her gold necklace and pearl earrings, among the most precious gifts she received from Alexander during their sixteen years of marriage. Alfons took his *siddur* and the book with the hard, green-colored cover that Ludwig had given him, among a few articles of clothing and some shoes.

Elsa also packed a single photo that Alexander had taken of her and the two children in their apartment soon after Helgi was born. Fearfully, she thought that if she ever became separated from her children, she would need the photograph to identify them.

## Chapter 7

In the backpack she wore, Elsa stuffed cloth diapers and rattles to help Helgi get through the sixteen-hour locomotive journey from Vienna to Paris. She was nervous that a crying baby would garner unnecessary attention from soldiers, but did not know how else to mitigate the needs of an infant child. In the backpack, she craftily wrapped whatever German Reichsmarks she had in the apartment in a lightly soiled diaper as a malodourous deterrent from any Nazis who checked their belongings before boarding or changing trains.

Elsa encouraged Alfons to rest for a few hours since they would need to rise early. Throughout the night, she kept a watchful eye over her two sleeping children, going over the exit permits that had been hastily prepared by their friend just to be sure everything appeared in order.

Elsa would miss their apartment, where she and Alexander grew from a young couple into a family. She knew that once they left, she would never see the inside again. She would never sit at the dining room table that they had inherited from her grandmother. She would never read a book on the living room couch, one of the first purchases she and Alexander made together after marrying. She would never prepare *Shabbat* dinner or Sunday breakfast from her kitchen.

All of those were possessions that could be replaced. Elsa was a woman of faith, and her belief in a benevolent God was seen through her daily routines and casual dialogue that made a strong impression on Alfons. Agreeing to move him from the Stern Yeshiva to the Gymnasium was one of the most difficult decisions she had made with Alexander. Elsa worried ending the formal Jewish education at the Stern Yeshiva could erode her son's practice of Jewish traditions and learning of Biblical texts. Young minds in those days were becoming more impressed with logic-driven principles in science and mathematics that was slowly encroaching on the need for faith and religion.

Alfons had promised his parents that he would observe the rituals on his own to alleviate their apprehension. He recited the daily prayers that he had learned at the Stern Yeshiva and ate only kosher food, even while tempted by the variety of lunch offerings at the Gymnasium that did not meet kosher guidelines. Alfons seemed more confident than his mother in his ability to follow these rituals, and his precociousness at ten years of age swayed Elsa to allow him to enroll in the highly selective preparatory school.

Elsa nudged Alfons reluctantly at six o'clock while he was still in a deep sleep, but they needed to leave for the central train station. Alfons wiped the slumber from his eyes. His mother explained that they would be facing a daunting journey through Germany and they would need to say goodbye to their home, their street and their city.

She evasively assured him they would return to make their departure easier, but Alfons was not convinced and was still hurting from the disappearance of Ludwig and his family. Nevertheless, Alfons knew that his mother and sister would need unwavering support over the next few days, and he was prepared to do whatever it took.

They walked down the five flights of steps carrying the three suitcases and two backpacks, while Elsa also carried Helgi in his arms. After a short wait, they signaled a taxicab in front of their apartment building to take them to the central train station. The sky was beginning to creep with light from the early rays of the sun and a slight chill borne between the transition of summer and autumn tingled their skin.

## Chapter 7

Elsa did not have the train schedule, but was hoping they could buy tickets and board the first train possible out of Vienna. This early in the morning, the station was not yet teeming with Nazi officers but there was enough of a German presence at the station that could potentially inspect their exit permits and disrupt their departure.

Alfons tended to his baby sister while his mother waited in the queue to purchase two one-way tickets to Paris. The emigration papers were legitimate, even if they were hastily prepared by Lowenherz. However, they had not calculated or paid the exit tax. An astute officer may realize that the dates on the emigration papers were signed less than a day before the family was actually leaving, making it nearly impossible to have settled the financial levy as the final hurdle to leave Austria.

They brought their suitcases and bags to the gate where a uniformed customs agent demanded to see their emigration papers. He would be the one to stamp their passports and provide the approval for them to leave the country. Alfons saw that the customs agent also had the swastika symbol adorned to his uniform sleeve. Creeping upon five months, baby Helgi had not yet eaten since being awoken earlier that morning and began to let her mother know it through her infant cries at the train station.

The uniformed customs agent fingered through the stack of papers that Elsa put on the table. As she returned her hands soothing Helgi, an inconspicuous whimper suddenly turned into an uncontrollable scream. The customs agent, displeased by the noise of the crying baby, tried to focus on the emigration papers. He looked up and asked in a firm manner, "Frau Sperber, where is the receipt of your exit tax payments?"

"I'm sorry, I could not... what did you ask me?"

## Live and Be Counted

The customs agent repeated his question in an alarming escalation. "I asked, Frau Sperber, where is receipt of your exit tax payments?"

Elsa purposefully appeared exacerbated by the distraction by her crying child and showed attempts to reach into her backpack for something to soothe Helgi. Elsa tried explaining their situation to the customs agent over Helgi's worsening cries.

"My husband," she stammered, trying to calm the baby at the same time. "My husband is remaining in Vienna and will be joining us in a week after he closes matters at home and pays the emigration tax."

The customs agent could barely hear Elsa's response and several people who had formed in line behind them were showing signs of impatience as the scene unfolded.

"Frau Sperber, I cannot hear you. I need you to show me payment of your exit tax."

Over the commotion, Elsa repeated that her husband was remaining in Vienna and was set to pay the emigration tax when he departed in a week.

The customs agent, not wanting to continue dealing with the vexing noise of the screaming baby and growing line of business travels, relented to the commotion and motioned Elsa and Alfons through the gate. A ticket taker punched their passes and pointed them in the direction of the tracks. They walked decisively to their departure track and waited for their outbound train to arrive.

With their tickets in hand and passports stamped, they breathed a sigh of relief when the passenger train began to pull away with Alfons, his mother and baby sister comfortably seated in a coach car. Alfons looked pensively out the window and

## Chapter 7

watched the city of his birth grow smaller as the locomotive train trudged away.

Pivotal memories chaotically swirled through his head. He thought about *Shabbat* meals with his aunts, uncles and cousins. What would happen to them?

He thought about his father's piano playing. Would they have a piano in their new home?

He could almost feel the wind blowing through his hair evoking memories from countryside joy rides in the Buick Century coupe. Would they have a car in Paris?

He replayed Herr Lowenherz's almost-cantorial rendering of the *Adon Olam* prayer from synagogue in his mind. Would they be able to go to *shul*?

He thought about running down the hallways at the Stern Yeshiva. Would he be able to make friends at his new school?

He smiled at the kindness of Herr Gerhart from the Gymnasium and felt his eyes well when he remembered Ludwig, his closest friend for as long as he could remember.

Alfons was a strong young man, dependable and staunch, but the losses from the only life he knew were innumerable. His eyes could no longer hold the small droplets that were collecting and tears began to run uncontrollably down his cheeks. He tried to keep his sobs as quiet as possible to avoid drawing any attention from passengers, but the tears kept flowing. He leaned to his left and buried his face in his mother's lap, and all she could do was stroke her hands across his head.

Eventually, Alfons lulled himself into a deep, exhausted sleep to the rickety sounds of the train tracks beneath him, his

## Live and Be Counted

head resting comfortably in her lap and his baby sister Helgi cozily cooing in her arms.

# Chapter 8

April 12, 2020

"Hi Papa!" Eli said rousingly as he opened the Zoom session following his last day of school before Passover break and spring recess. It was also weighing on Eli's mind that his immigration project was due to his teacher when they were scheduled to return to school. While he had been listening in fascination and suspense about Papa's clandestine escape from Austria, he still did not know how Papa came to America.

"I'm helping my parents clean out all the *chametz* for the holiday, referring to the grain-type foods prohibited to eat on Passover and symbolic of the unrisen flatbreads called *matzah* that the ancient Israelites ate during the Exodus from Egyptian slavery. "It's going to be sad not being with you and Grandma Phyllis for the holiday."

Just over a month since the coronavirus was declared a global pandemic, schools and parks were still closed and social distancing was the new term, signaling the need to maintain six feet from anyone outside the immediate family.

Little League baseball was already canceled, restaurants turned to take-out only and grocery stores made customers wait outside when it reached a maximum number of shoppers. Everyone was wearing masks and some of the homemade ones began to reflect the creativity and personality of its wearer.

Eli watched his parents work from their laptops at home, his father at the desk in the master bedroom and his mother at the dining room table, closest to where he was stationed in the den.

## Live and Be Counted

His two older siblings took their virtual classes from their bedrooms upstairs, and it wasn't unusual to only see them emerge for mealtimes. Eli appreciated the rediscovery of board games with his siblings on *Shabbat* afternoon.

All the community rabbis declared that synagogues would remain closed during Passover, and more alarmingly, warned against extended families gathering to celebrate the holiday together.

"Grandma Phyllis and I are not taking any chances. We have most of our things delivered to us, including medicine and groceries. You can buy almost everything online!"

"Papa, I'm impressed you do your shopping online. You're really with the times, I don't know any great grandfathers who use Amazon or Doordash!" Eli remarked.

"Door-who?" Papa asked, which sent Eli into a hysterical laugher.

"You know Papa, I was thinking that Passover is all about the Jewish people's freedom from slavery," Eli captured the essence of the story in a short statement. "How can it be that we're forced to stay at home and can't celebrate with our families? What type of freedom is that?"

It was hard for Alfons to disagree. He and Phyllis would be celebrating the holiday by themselves without their families from either side. He was reflecting about Passovers some eighty years before which he spent alone, hidden away and separated from his parents and sister.

"Some people are calling the coronavirus the eleventh plague," Eli said referring to the ten plagues that highlight the central Passover story with which God struck the ancient Egyptians to force their release of the Israelites from more than two hundred

## Chapter 8

years of slavery. "I suppose it will take another miracle from God to end the virus."

"Right now, God is giving our scientists the knowledge and tools to develop a vaccine," Papa said assuredly. "We just have to be patient."

"It makes you wonder why God would even bring a virus like this in the first place," Eli said with a hint of anger, although tried not to appear that he was judgmentally questioning the ways of God.

"Why God brings pain and suffering to people is one of man's greatest challenges of faith," Papa almost retreated given the complexity of this topic for a ten-year old, but decided to tread lightly and see where it would go.

"The painful things that happen to us are not punishments for our misbehavior. I've never felt betrayed or abandoned by God when tragedy strikes or when we experience unspeakable pain. In those moments, and there have been many moments in my lifetime, I have turned to God even more for help in getting through."

Eli lingered for several long seconds to formulate his thoughts and asked, "Is that how you survived the Holocaust?"

"Throughout the years of running and hiding from the Nazis, I never lost my faith in God. I didn't always understand why it was happening, but I looked to God for reassurance and guidance."

Papa shifted the topic slightly, "You know Eli, this isn't the first time the world has faced a health pandemic like this. Exactly one hundred years ago we had the Spanish Flu."

## Live and Be Counted

"Really?" Eli asked. "You mean this has happened before? How did it end?"

Alfons himself wasn't all that sure about the origins and effects of the Spanish Flu. Most of what he knew was from recent newspaper articles that were drawing comparisons to COVID-19.

He related to Eli that the Spanish Flu lasted about two years from 1918 and 1920. There was no effective treatment or vaccines and people were told to wear masks. Many schools, theaters and businesses shuttered and, even back then, people were asked to social distance. Despite that, more than fifty million people around the world died.

"Eventually the Spanish Flu went away because people who contracted and recovered from the virus also developed a future immunity to it," Papa said.

"Hold on a minute," Eli interjected. "It sounds exactly like what's happening today in 2020. With no vaccine, the only way we can move forward from COVID-19 is for everyone to get it."

"Some of the infectious disease experts are talking about *herd immunity*, where the majority of people recover from the virus and develop antibodies to fight off secondary infections," Papa iterated. "The virus doesn't disappear, instead populations build a collective immunity to it and slow its spread." Alfons thought to himself that sadly many people will not be able to fight off the virus as society builds toward herd immunity.

Eli liked that solution to end the pandemic. He already knew several teachers and parents of his friends who became infected with COVID-19, and all of them seemed to recover from it in due time. He was hearing about the mounting death toll, but the possibility of a family member or relative of a close friend that he knew personally not surviving the virus seemed remote to him.

## Chapter 8

Suddenly his mind shifted gears. "Papa, wait. Didn't you tell me that The Great War ended in 1918? Isn't that the same time that the Spanish Flu started? Was this some type of biological weapon that Spain created to fight in The Great War?"

"That is some theory, Eli!" Papa considered if science in the early part of the 1900s was advanced enough to even conceive such an idea.

"I actually read that the Spanish Flu did not originate in Spain. During The Great War, Spain was a neutral country and its journalists were free to cover events of the war without censorship. Governments of countries that were involved in the fighting largely controlled what was being reported by their newspapers and tried to cover up the spread of the flu as a way of keeping high morale with their soldiers and citizens. Because Spanish news sources were the only ones reporting on it, many people around the world believed it originated there and called it the Spanish Flu."

Eli's mind was wondering if there was a deeper connection. He minimized the Zoom screen on his iPad and opened a Google search bar where he typed *Spanish Flu and World War One*. Eagerly, he read the first paragraph of the first link that appeared in the search results.

"Papa, listen to this!" he jumped excitedly. "The conditions during World War One were so bad that the disease spread rapidly throughout Europe, especially among soldiers on both sides. The flu actually helped bring the countries together to end the war."

"I did not know that," Papa was genuinely intrigued.

"There's more," Eli persisted. "During the peace negotiations in France, President Wilson and the American delegation was opposed to Germany paying reparations to the other countries since they felt it was better for everyone to look forward. However, many from the American delegation, including President Wilson himself, got sick from the flu at the start of the peace negotiations, resulting in England and France succeeding in their demands that Germany be responsible to pay reparations to the countries that were most affected by their actions."

"Eli, that's very interesting." Papa was enjoying this short history lesson. "And to think that if the American delegation did not get infected with the flu in 1918, a different treaty might have been signed without Germany paying reparations."

"I remember you told me about reparations, money Germany needed to pay other countries to rebuild from the damage it inflicted during World War One," Eli recalled, pleased with himself for remembering its meaning.

"That's right," Papa continued. "The reparations were among the reasons Germany's economy sank during the 1920s and 1930s. Among the promises that Hitler made to the Germans was to restore the prosperity that was lost after Germany was forced to pay reparations in the treaty that ended World War One," Papa reminded him.

Eli considered a final thought to himself. If the Spanish Flu hadn't sickened the American delegation and Germany had not been required to pay reparations, is it possible that Hitler would not have risen to power and there would not have been a World War Two?

# Part Two

**Northern France**

## Chapter 9

September 1938

The train carrying Alfons, his mother Elsa and his sister Helgi made more than a dozen uneventful stops in cities across Austria, Germany and France on its way to Paris. At several stops, train officials asked to see travel tickets and passports, including the stop at Munich, which Alfons noted was crawling with German soldiers. Everything was in order and their presence on the train and paperwork they carried did not raise any suspicion.

Alfons shared the time with his mother holding baby Helgi, sometimes walking up and down the passenger aisle with a slight bounce as he cradled her in his arms. Elsa purchased a scotch and dabbed one of the handkerchiefs with alcohol for Helgi to suck on when she became irritable and showed signs of crying. It was a technique that was common at the turn of the twentieth century. While she grew skeptical of the practice having learned it from her own mother after Alfons was born, this was a desperate time and she did so unapologetically.

"What are you reading?" his mother glanced over Alfons' shoulder after he pulled a hard covered book with a green color from his backpack.

"It's called *The Hobbit*," he answered. "Ludwig gave it to me for my birthday last March. I never got a chance to read it. It has more than 300 pages, so it's a little intimidating. The book was written by John Tolkien from England and it's about a heroic Halfling's quest to find a treasure being guarded by a dragon."

"Alfons, put the book away. Quickly!" his mother pleaded.

## Live and Be Counted

"Why can't I read the book, Mother?" he protested. "It's a long train ride and this will help me pass the time. Ludwig told me that the story was inspired by the author's experiences during The Great War when he served in the British army."

"Please Alfons," his mother repeated sternly this time, in as much as a hushed tone that she could. "Tolkien has been very outspoken of the Nazi party. He's called them pernicious racists in British newspapers. If any of the German conductors see you reading the book, they may… I don't want to think about it. Just put it away."

"Mother, I was looking forward to reading it."

"How did Ludwig obtain a copy that he gave to you, anyway?" she asked curiously. Elsa had heard that Germany refused to translate the original English copy into German when the book became instantly popular with children.

"I'm not sure," Alfons admitted. He also did not know any of the political background behind the book. "Maybe Ludwig's father brought it home after one of his business trips to London, before they disappeared."

Grudgingly closing the cover and slipping it into his backpack, Alfons clung to the book sensing the wicked irony that the gift from Ludwig could get him into trouble with the Nazis. As the two boys found themselves simultaneously in the crosshairs of the Gestapo, a simple novel, mythical of sorts, was serving as a defiant gesture against the German oppression. It remained the only physical link Alfons had back to his best friend as he was fleeing from his home.

Maybe just maybe, Alfons thought, Ludwig and his family escaped Austria and went to London, just as he was fleeing with his family to Paris.

## Chapter 9

Time on the train continued to pass uneventfully with optimistic chatter between Alfons and his mother about what better life would bring them in Paris. New schools, green parks, enlivened streets, and most importantly relief from the daily fear of the Gestapo they had come to live with since the *Anschluss*. Except for the little French that Alfons had begun to learn at the Gymnasium, he would feel helpless in his new classrooms.

"You're just going to do the best that you can," his mother comforted him. "We'll find you a tutor and get you extra help."

It had been about two months since they had seen Father, and with each roll of the steel wheels beneath them, anticipation grew toward their reunion. Alfons gazed out the windows as the train passed through long stretches of undeveloped farm land and unkempt fields. Most looked uninhabited but there were occasional barns and cottages that he surmised were owned by farmers who supplied the cities with food. The skies were clear blue in September and, to him, signaled calmness and tranquility that awaited them in Paris.

It was morning when the conductors walked up the aisles and woke the passengers who were still asleep from the night. The Gare du Nord in Paris, which had opened in 1866 with thirty-six platforms, was the final destination of their journey and the busiest railway station in Europe. Alfons carefully treaded down three steps of the train with two suitcases in hand and a backpack over his shoulders. He breathlessly looked up at the triumphal arches that made up the grand station's facade and lent a hand to his mother who was holding Helgi as she applied equal caution walking down onto solid ground.

Alfons clutched his mother's hand tightly, in awe of the hundreds, maybe thousands of people who were walking in every which way to catch their trains to work or arriving in France's capital from the outer cities. They looked at each other's eyes with

## Live and Be Counted

a collective sense of achievement, but no words needed to be spoken. His mother nodded and the three of them took the first steps from the platform into their new life in Paris.

They followed the *Sortie* signs to leave the main terminal. Even from the Gymnasium, Alfons knew that meant *Exit*. He was going to have to be a quick study of French language if he was going to make it in Paris. They entered the queue for the taxicabs and waited a short five minutes before a dispatcher with a whistle guided them into a yellow car. Elsa reached into the front pocket of the backpack that she was carrying and unfolded a small white piece of paper.

"Rue Lafayette, *s'il vous plaît*," she said to the driver.

"How come Father wasn't here to meet us?" Alfons asked as the taxicab pulled away. It had been about two months since he had seen his father and had hoped to meet him at the train station.

"My dear, Father doesn't even know we left Vienna," his mother said. "He thinks we are still there. He doesn't know the Gestapo found out about the payments he was redirecting to Paris all these months. Our friend Josef Lowenherz, who was working for Eichmann and the Gestapo, was able to prepare exit visas for us to leave in such a haste. Your father sent me a letter with the return address on the envelope and that's why I know where he has been living."

"What did Father say in the letter?" Alfons was curious, but also perturbed his father had not written him a letter.

"Actually, he didn't say much in the letter," his mother explained. "He was very careful not to provide any facts that he was in Paris or preparing to bring us there to live. In case the letter was intercepted by the Gestapo in Vienna, he purposefully spoke only of the business and procurement of materials he was bringing

## Chapter 9

back to Austria. The most important element of the letter was not what was inside, but what was written on the envelope. 18 Rue Lafayette."

Paris was just starting its day and people of all types – students, shop owners, street cleaners – were embarking on their morning routines. Alfons looked out of the window and marveled how the rising sun shined brightly on the cobblestone streets and against some of the large, stone buildings.

Everything seemed relatively normal.

The taxi drive took about thirty-five minutes, winding out of the narrow streets of the heavily bustling city center of Paris and passing through neighborhoods that had a more suburban feel with parks and trees hugging the banks of the Seine River. When they arrived, Alfons jumped out of the cab and skipped ahead as his mother delicately brought Helgi from the backseat. He looked back at his mother for nodding approval and Alfons heart raced as he firmly pressed his finger on the gently lit buzzer to 18 Rue Lafayette.

From the top floor of the two-story building, Alexander peeled back the curtain suspiciously, not expecting visitors at this hour. One of his buyers owned the space above the retail store in the shopping district of Chelles on the eastern outskirts of Paris. At the time, it was being used mostly for storage of unsold, returned or out-of-style jackets, a portion of which came from the Sperber's sewing floor in Vienna. It had been originally built as a two-bedroom apartment equipped with heating and plumbing that would be comfortable for a family of four.

Matching smiles adorned both their faces when the door opened and Alfons embraced his father for the first time in two months. "I knew you would make it!" Alexander joyfully announced. "Not a single doubt in my mind. I just didn't know when."

He let Alfons land back on his feet and walked toward his wife, who was holding Helgi. "Oh my, how she has grown," he said lifting the baby into the air. "Two months isn't that long, but when you're only five months old, it's almost half a lifetime!"

Alfons laughed heartily at his father's humor and was swept with relief to be together again in Paris, safe from the Nazis. There would be new challenges for all of them, but those were surmountable so long as they had each other and did not need to run.

Over the coming weeks, Elsa and Alexander organized the apartment into a homey space. It wasn't as spacious as their apartment in Vienna, and it didn't have any of their familiar furnishings or pictures, but it was home. Alfons shared a bedroom with his sister, who always awoke a few hours earlier than he would have liked. Each morning, his mother retrieved Helgi from her crib, bringing the baby into her bed so that Alfons could sleep a little longer before getting ready for school.

For the time being, he felt protected and safe.

Three months into their resettlement, they received a letter from their aunt and uncle who lived across the street in Vienna. They related how the Gestapo came to the Sperbers' apartment with a warrant just hours after Alfons, his mother and Helgi fled the city. They described Huber and Eichmann being furious that they had slipped through their fingers and got out before they could be arrested.

In the letter, Alfons' aunt and uncle lamented how the situation in Vienna was growing worse for the Jews with deportations increasing, not just to the Dachau camp in Germany, but also to cities in Poland, the names of which he did not recognize.

His uncle continued to recount a most horrific night in November where Nazis torched synagogues, destroyed Jewish cemeteries and shattered the windows of Jewish businesses. The events were referred to as *Kristallnacht,* the night of broken glass, which resulted in the death of nearly one hundred Jews, either directly at the hands of the Nazis or from the burning fires as they tried to save precious assets and religious articles.

Alfons read in Paris' Jewish newspaper *Naye Prese* a month earlier about similar events being reported from Berlin. He stood disbelievingly as his father read the letter that described coordinated efforts to terrorize the Jews in Vienna in a similar night of destruction. His uncle wrote about Nazis setting ablaze most of Vienna's synagogues and throwing rocks through the windows of Jewish stores. The Stern Yeshiva was burned to a shell as the fire department looked on, ready to intervene only if the fire threatened neighboring buildings. Jewish infrastructure, investment, and way of life was ruthlessly ravaged and decimated in a single night of terror.

Alfons and his family escaped Vienna as the Nazis were strengthening their grip and bringing anguish to the Jewish communities. The letter was the last time Alfons heard from any of his extended family who remained behind.

# Chapter 10

April 20, 2020

"Hi Papa!" Eli waved eagerly as his Zoom picture came into focus. It had been over month since Eli began the chats with his great grandfather. They didn't happen every day, but they usually didn't skip more than a few in a row. April's showers were giving way to the warming temperatures of spring, and Eli was finding himself outdoors in the backyard with the next-door neighbors.

"Yesterday, we had a big water fight with water guns and water balloons. By far, I had the best weapon. I used the hose from the side of the house to spray everyone down!" Eli said thrillingly. He was pretty sure that his wet clothes were still laying on his bedroom floor and made a mental note to hang them in the bathroom.

"Aren't you supposed to be social distancing with your friends? How did you have water fight?" Papa asked with concern.

"Papa!" Eli could not get the words out quick enough. "An outdoor water fight is the perfect social distancing activity to do with friends. We were well more than six feet apart with our water guns and we each ran back to our own houses to fill water balloons. I can't wait to do it again tomorrow! Did you ever have water fights with your friends when you were growing up?"

There was a long, uncomfortable pause and Eli watched Papa turn his head away from the screen, saddened that his question might have sparked poignant memories for Papa.

## Chapter 10

"As a matter of fact, I did," he finally said, returning his face to the center of the screen. "Ludwig and I used to play in a park with other friends near the Danube River not far from where we lived. After school ended in June, the city workers who helped run the park turned on a fountain that all the kids used to cool down during the hot summer months. We didn't have water guns, but we used our hands and pails to splash water on each other."

Eli's excitement grew over the commonality between him and his great grandfather. It was sometimes hard for Eli to imagine Papa as a young boy of ten or eleven years old, as himself.

"I also used to leave my wet clothing on the floor when I came home!" to which they both laughed at the irony of having similar fun more than eighty years apart and half a world away.

"Papa, tell me what Paris was like? Was it as romantic as they make it in the movies?" Eli was running through the Disney library in his mind, recalling a handful of movies like Ratatouille, Madeline and Hunchback of Notre Dame that were all set in Paris.

"Paris was a beautiful city, it still is. We lived in a small neighborhood on the eastern part of the city called Chelles, where other Jewish immigrants had settled, many of them from Germany and Austria. There were kosher grocery shops and Jewish bookstores. Our neighbors were friendly and we made the very best of our new lives. Father invested in the business he had already restarted in Paris and worked hard to expand his network of suppliers and buyers throughout the country."

"Did you go back to school?" Eli wondered how Papa was spending his time, if he was needed in the store or if he could return to being a normal child.

"We arrived in Paris in September, just after schools had started. My parents enrolled me in the public school nearby, but everything was taught in French and the little French I had been

## Live and Be Counted

picking up at the Gymnasium was not enough to get me through the sixth grade. My parents sent me to an after-school language class to accelerate my French and hired a tutor on the weekends who helped me with my homework."

"What about synagogue, did you go to *shul* on *Shabbat*?" Eli felt like he was interviewing his great grandfather. In a way he was.

"Father and I resumed going to the synagogue in our neighborhood, not just on *Shabbat,* but for morning services during the week as well. The synagogue in Paris was nearly identical to our synagogue in Vienna more than a thousand kilometers away. I could read Hebrew well, so following the prayer services in Paris came very easy. Even as the Jewish people have been spread all over the world, our religious practices are almost the same everywhere. Sure, there are some differences as customs evolve or Jewish traditions take on the flavor of local surroundings, but you can go almost anywhere in the world where Jews are living and fall right into place with familiar customs."

Eli concurred. "One time I went on vacation to the beach with my parents and siblings. About a mile from our hotel was a synagogue we walked to for *Shabbat* services. The rabbi invited us to stay for dinner and the entire evening followed the same routine I was used to back home."

"You see? It's true," Papa reassured him. "Almost anywhere you go in the world, Jews observe the traditions in almost the same ways."

Alfons reflected how his parents made friends quickly and felt welcomed in Paris, occasionally invited to other families for *Shabbat* lunch in the way they used to host guests in Vienna. Father's raincoat and sportswear business was growing at an acceptable rate given his need to start over. For the most part,

## Chapter 10

their lives were resuming normalcy and they did not have to worry about being harassed by the Gestapo.

Eli was relieved that Papa and his family had escaped from the Nazis in Austria, and speculated why they came to the United States if they were living peacefully in Paris. He decided to hold back his question, certain it would be answered in time.

Papa resumed. "While attending a public school in Paris, I continued my Hebrew and Judaic studies with a community rabbi that Father hired and when I turned twelve in March 1939, the rabbi spent the next year preparing me for my *Bar Mitzvah*. He taught me to read my *Torah* portion with the traditional melodic notes, like most thirteen-year-old boys are expected to do in the synagogue."

Eli continued to be astounded. "It's amazing that you were preparing for your *Bar Mitzvah* eighty years ago, the same way that Jewish children continue to do today."

"This tradition dates back two thousand years!" Papa explained. "Some of the melodies have developed over time in different parts of the world, but the similarities they share and meaning conveyed by the melody is common to all traditions."

"Do you remember the melody for your *Torah* portion?" Eli asked. He recalled his older brother spending a year studying for his *Bar Mitzvah* and looked forward when he would start learning his own.

"No, I don't," Papa replied with a small hint of regret. "I know when my *Torah* portion is scheduled to be read each year, but I don't remember how to read it at all."

Eli's eyes peered at the calendar that was tacked to the wall near the computer desk at which he was sitting. "We've missed six weeks of *Torah* portions since the coronavirus lockdown. I wonder if we will have to make up all the missed portions when we're allowed to return, or if we'll just continue with the current week's scheduled reading."

"Actually, the *Torah* portion from my *Bar Mitzvah* was read in March on the last *Shabbat* before we had to quarantine," Papa recounted with surprise. Eli could see Papa moving his lips and counting on his fingers, performing some type of mental calculation. "And this past March was exactly the eightieth anniversary of my own *Bar Mitzvah* which I celebrated in Paris."

"What was your *Bar Mitzvah* like, Papa?" Eli asked. "Did you have a big party with music and dancing, chocolate desserts, balloons and a photographer?"

"Not quite, Eli." Papa said reflexively. "It was March 1940 when I read my *Torah* portion in the synagogue. German fighter planes were roaring overhead and bombs could be heard falling in the near distance."

# Chapter 11

September 1939 – March 1940

In their apartment in the Chelles district on the western outskirts of Paris, Alfons' parents kept a radio in the living room that the three of them would listen to together at night after Helgi was put to bed. Like many households, the radio box became a central piece of furniture surrounded by sitting chairs so that everyone from the family could crowd around to hear the latest installment of their favorite show. Radio had such mass appeal because it united communities of people, virtually from their homes.

From the crackling sound of the Westinghouse radio box, they would often tune into to the Radio Paris station, which was the most popular among Parisians. Alfons liked listening to music, but he also enjoyed the game shows and storytelling that came from the broadcasts. In the 1930s, radio had reached a new audience appeal with Adolf Hitler's rising popularity. Europeans' enjoyment of musical entertainment was increasing interrupted with breaking news from Berlin. It was the first diplomatic crisis to be played out on the airwaves, reaching nearly every household.

Some journalists and politicians referred to the early years of Germany occupation as a 'bloodless conquest' since radio could win the hearts and minds of people as the crisis moved on at a lightning pace. Through this new media channel, the Nazis controlled the message vibrating into people's homes. Early on, they were successful in convincing most Austrians that *Anschluss* was a good thing for them. With the breakneck speed of events also defined by the new culture of instant communication, radio helped to write history as it was unfolding.

## Live and Be Counted

In Paris, Alexander devoted his efforts to growing the business while Elsa took care of Helgi and the home. He traveled to cities across France, such as Bordeaux, Lyon and Toulouse, to expand his supplier network and kept his trips short whenever possible to be home for *Shabbat* with the family. Alfons started seventh grade In September 1939, absorbed himself in schoolwork and preparing for his *Bar Mitzvah*. So much of the prior school year felt like a blur as he was still learning the foundations of French. He was proud of the progress he had made and committed himself to excelling as best as he could in the upcoming school year.

On a clear night, and with the right angle of the antenna, the Sperbers could get reception from German and British broadcasts providing updates on the developments of the war. It was possible to hear entirely different perspectives on the same event depending which broadcast they received. When they could only tune into Radio Paris, Alfons was often called by his parents to help translate what he could.

The Sperber routine continued as the early stages of the war played out to them in a virtual way. When they listened to the radio, Alfons tried to imagine the front speaker as a security fence separating the serenity in his home from the ominous voice of the Westinghouse that was describing escalating hostilities between France and Germany. In Paris, in 1939, Alfons could simply end the conflict by turning off the radio and ignoring its transmission.

Having lived through the *Anschluss* in Austria and experienced the growing hatred of Jews by the German occupiers, Alfons' felt confident in the life they were rebuilding in Paris. Jewish presence in France dated back to the fifth century and had become a center for Jewish observance and scholarship in the Middle Ages. Anti Semitism had occurred in cycles, but Parisian Jews, especially those with deep generational links to France, largely enjoyed freedoms for academic, economic and religious

## Chapter 11

pursuits. France had its share of Nazi sympathizers and Hitler supporters, but it had not grown into a systemic order and French Jews, much like Alfons and his family, felt they were on the safe side of the fence with Germany.

Alfons had cornered himself in the living room after dinner to complete his math homework, away from Helgi who, at eighteen-months old, was cruising around the room using furniture to balance her footing. Alfons turned the radio volume high enough to signal anything important, but still low enough to avoid distraction as he plugged away at his assignment. The urgency in the newsflash musical tones was enough to grab his attention.

"Father! Mother!" Papa called from the living room. He was gently turning the dial to eliminate any interference that was coming in from the transmission, putting his ear to the speaker to pick up every word. "They're saying that Germany invaded Poland, and that France and England have declared war on Germany together."

"It's about time," Alexander replied with a bit of hope in his voice. "Nazi Germany has been operating without any resistance and no country was mounting a worthy defense against the onslaught."

Alfons continued translating the broadcast as best he could. "They are saying that Germany sunk a British cruise ship off the coast of Ireland killing over one hundred passengers, and that France is mobilizing soldiers to defend against German aggressions on the eastern front."

Alexander's voice grew with eagerness that Germany would begin facing pressure to pull its soldiers back. "With France and England now coming to the defense of Poland and

## Live and Be Counted

Czechoslovakia, surely this will bring this senseless tyranny to an end," he hopefully predicted.

Over the next several weeks, they listened intently to the radio for updates on the war. Elsa brought hot tea and French biscuits to the radio box in the living room, comfort food which helped reassure Alfons in these times of uncertainty. England was imposing a naval blockade of shipping lanes on Germany's coastline in the North Sea and France was moving its soldiers toward its eastern border near Saarbrucken.

Both efforts, however, failed to halt Germany's advancement. The artillery brought by England and France proved to be slow and less sophisticated than that of Germany, with many of England's naval carriers in the Black Sea torpedoed by German airplanes. The French army largely retreated from whatever small territorial gains they had made when they encountered a forest filled with exploding mines planted by the German army. Large cities in Poland such as Krakow, Lodz and Warsaw capitulated to the Nazis. By October 1939, talk was circulating among French social and political circles that Germany was preparing a military offensive against France.

While aspects of the war unfolded, Alfons continued his inexorable march to Jewish adulthood and met weekly with his rabbi. Alfons worked hard to prepare for the scriptural *Torah* portion he would chant at the synagogue, the blessings he would recite and the black leather straps of the *t'fillin* he would don. When his father reminded him to review the cantillations, Alfons knew in his heart he was doing what any father would, even if the constant reminders irritated him just a bit.

His parents were planning to host a small dessert for the congregation at the synagogue after *Shabbat* services to celebrate the *Bar Mitzvah* occasion, so Alfons knew the spotlight would be

## Chapter 11

on him.  As a gift for reaching this important achievement, his parents presented him with a French Cartier watch.

It was March 1940, Alfons was reviewing the final pieces of his *Bar Mitzvah* recital.  The winter was preparing its thaw to the cooler temperatures of spring.  Germany was preparing for its invasion of France.

Alexander received an enlistment order from the government and was now preparing to mobilize into the French Army.

# Chapter 12

May 1, 2020

"Papa, many kids in the neighborhood had their *Bar Mitzvah*'s canceled because of COVID-19," Eli said at the start of their next Zoom session. "They studied their *Torah* portion for an entire year and their *Bar Mitzvah* couldn't happen because the synagogues were closed."

"Sure, their celebration parties were canceled, but they were still able to reach their *Bar Mitzvah*, the age at which they are inducted as an adult in Jewish ways of life."

Eli told Papa how families were replacing *Bar Mitzvah* celebrations with *Car Mitzvah* parties, explaining the procession of vehicles honking their horns as they passed by the Bar Mitzvah boy's home, sometimes joined by the shrieking sirens of police cars and fire trucks.

Papa smiled at the creative ways of filling lifecycle voids resulting from social distancing rules.

Suddenly, Grandma Phyllis called from the other room listening in on the conversation. "I supposed that for any other age you can make a birthday *carty*. Al, if we're still doing this next March, I'm going to make you a surprise *carty*!" They all laughed in unison and suggested all sorts of ways they would bring Papa to the party under the veil of surprise.

"Papa, tell me more about what it was like around your *Bar Mitzvah*," Eli brought them from the coronavirus back to 1940.

## Chapter 12

Alfons reached back into his memory bank turning thirteen and recounted the reconnaissance flights and bombing raids between France, England and Germany. Germany had already occupied Belgium, Luxembourg and Holland in 1940 with very little resistance and it was widely feared they would attempt to invade France as well.

Like rolling seven or higher in Risk, Eli thought again to himself.

"The French needed able-bodied men to fight against the Germans, and many adult men were drafted to the French Army. Soon after my *Bar Mitzvah* in April 1940, Father was forced to enlist too."

"Grandpa Alexander fought in World War Two?" Eli asked dubiously. He never knew anyone who was an actual soldier.

"He was drafted into the army, but wasn't quite a soldier. He had no prior military experience, so they put him in a battalion without arms."

"What do you mean *without arms*?" Eli asked. "Surely you don't mean…" he paused short of offering a gruesome explanation which he knew couldn't be possible.

"To be in the military *without arms* is to work in an area that supports soldiers on the frontline rather than actually carrying a weapon," Papa interceded. "I'm not quite sure what exactly my father did and his time in the French military was very short, anyway."

In May 1940, three million German soldiers had amassed at France's northwestern borders with Holland, Belgium and Luxembourg after Germany had occupied the northern countries.

## Live and Be Counted

"Germany's ambition to control France was largely motivated to confront any attempts of a counterattack from England or the US which would likely come from the Atlantic Ocean or from across the English Channel," Papa continued. "On May 10, 1940, German soldiers used an air campaign to clear the way and overpowered French soldiers on the ground. A little more than a month later, the French surrendered and entered an armistice treaty that basically divided France in half. The northern part of France fell under German control and the southern part remained governed by the French, but under the scrutiny of the Nazis."

Alfons had heard that the Nazis seized two million prisoners from the French army and sent them to labor camps across France and Germany. The Jewish prisoners had been sorted and sent to the harshest of camps where many died of malnutrition, disease and harsh weather.

"What happened to Grandpa Alexander?" Eli asked.

"Father was rounded up with other soldiers and taken prisoner. There were many men in our neighborhood who were also taken as prisoners and never returned to their families. Once again, it was just Mother, me and Helgi and it would not be safe to remain in Paris with the German occupation."

"Where did you go?"

"First, we went to Bordeaux which is a large city on France's western side along the Atlantic Coast. We were there for two weeks before making our way to Toulouse, a large city in the southeast of France."

Eli put up his hand, "Wait, Papa! I want to see where Bordeaux and Toulouse are." He shared his Zoom screen with Papa as he brought up a map of France from his search bar. Papa guided Eli's finger to the bottom part of the map. "Google Maps says it

## Chapter 12

takes six hours to drive from Paris to Bordeaux. That doesn't seem like such a long trip to do at once."

"Actually, it took about three days to travel from Paris to Bordeaux," Papa said without a bit of hesitation in his voice. "It was a long and difficult journey, one which I will never forget."

"As Father was taken into the French army, he warned Mother to take whatever she could and make her way to Toulouse. Father had a business contact who managed distribution of his raincoats across Toulouse and neighboring villages. Father implored Mother to find his contact. He gave Mother a few hundred Francs that he had saved from the business and hid in their apartment. He also told her where money was hidden at the store."

"Grandpa Alexander always seemed to have a plan," Eli resolved.

"Father was a smart businessman and his mind was always planning ahead. However, we did not know how to get to Toulouse. Mother had a widowed friend who had access to a horse and carriage she used to deliver milk from farm on the outskirts of the city. She told Mother that she was going to Bordeaux where she had a married son and that the three of us could leave the city with her. In that moment, we didn't have much of a choice."

"I can't believe this is the second time in two years you needed to go on the run," Eli said astonishingly.

"It was also the second time we fled without my father to lead us," Papa said. "He had promised that he would meet up with us as soon as he could, but in my heart I was wrapped with fear of never seeing him again."

# Chapter 13

Early May 1940

"Alfons dear," his mother cried to him from across the apartment. "We need to pack again. We're leaving in the morning."

This time, there was no uncle to help them, no certainty about where they were going or who might meet them when they arrived. The last vision of his father in a distinguished French uniform masked an uneasiness that neither Alfons nor his mother were able to admit. Alexander was now on the frontline of the war as a French soldier without arms.

He was vulnerable, he was untrained and he was Jewish.

Headlines had already reached the French press reporting on Germany's swift conquest of Holland, Luxembourg and Belgium. There was little military resistance and the Nazis had rounded up many of the Jews living in the large cities, almost too easily. What they were doing with them, Alfons did not know. Surely, it was too far to send entire Jewish communities to places like Dachau where Ludwig's family had most likely been sent.

Alfons slept restlessly, not wanting to uproot again. He was enjoying Paris, its gothic-like buildings, its narrow streets clearly not built for the advent of cars, the Seine River which reminded him of the Danube in Vienna. He was even taken by its culture and history, even though it was not his place of birth.

"Mother, no one else here is leaving. Why do we need to?" he asked her in the morning.

## Chapter 13

"Alfons," she said, "the Jews who have lived here for generations are safe. They are French Jews and the Germans aren't after them. They are part of the French culture, speak the French language and are contributors to the French society. Many of them wore the French uniform and served in The Great War. The French Jews have the protection of the French government."

"The government would just hand us to the Germans, even though we've been living here, going to school here and working here? We've never done anything wrong, we've never broken any laws," Alfons protested.

"The French take pride in their culture, in their history and in their traditions," Elsa responded. "Many of them have not been happy with the influx of Jewish immigrants coming from other countries over the past several years. They fear that immigrants will take jobs away from the French, especially as unemployment continues to rise. I fear that the French, without hesitation, would sacrifice the immigrant Jews to the Germans to protect themselves.

Alfons was disturbed by what he was hearing. The last two years in Paris had been peaceful and quiet. At first, it was hard to adjust to their new surroundings, but they were succeeding in rebuilding their life together. Alfons went back to his room reluctantly and started packing clothing into his bag, more callously this time. Leaving Vienna was hard, but even while they were fleeing from their home, Alfons also knew that his father was waiting for them when they arrived. Now they were fleeing their home in Paris and leaving his father behind.

Nothing felt right.

"Do you have your things?" his mother beseeched from across the room, acting with a bit more urgency knowing their ride would not wait. "We're going with Helena Bensimon, my friend from down the street. She has no children left at home and her husband was also called into the French Civil Corps. Helena is going to Bordeaux where her son lives and she said we can ride with her."

"How long will it take us to get to Bordeaux?" he asked.

"The trip is about six hundred kilometers," his mother said, holding something back. "The Germans are headed to France and we need to stay one step ahead of them. I packed bread, hard boiled eggs and some fruit. We'll get out and find places to drink water."

Alfons could hear the anxiety rising in his mother's voice and the urgency made him wonder if she knew something that she was not sharing with him. He felt that he should know what they were up against if they were going to flee from Paris.

After all, Alfons was thirteen years old and Jewish tradition considered him old enough to carry all its responsibilities. He was the only man in the family right now and felt a growing duty to protect his mother and sister. It occurred to him that maybe his mother didn't have a plan that was fully thought through. Alfons saw that she was scared and feared that she was acting rashly.

They finished packing their bags. Elsa tucked her gold jewelry and the picture of Alfons holding Helgi from Vienna into the inside pocket of the backpack. They met up with Helena at the end of the street and walked seven blocks toward the center of Chelles, Helgi in Elsa's arms and Alfons tugging the bags. Elsa waived to a taxicab that was parked at the corner and motioned everyone to hop in.

"*Bonjour*," she greeted the driver. "We need to make a quick stop at the shop on Rue Lafayette." Turning to Alfons she said, "Then Helena will direct us to the farm where her husband keeps the horse and carriage he uses for his deliveries. That's how we're getting to Bordeaux."

## Chapter 13

Did he hear correctly? A horse and carriage? It was 1942 and the modern way of travel was by car or bus. How long would the journey take? What would they eat and where would they sleep? Questions flooded his mind, but Alfons heard the decisiveness in his mother's voice. Rather than creating doubt in her plan, Alfons knew that for his mother and sister's sake he needed to replace his own trepidation with confidence. They would get through this together.

When the taxicab arrived fifteen minutes later at his father's shop, Elsa jumped out of the cab with her backpack still on and saw two women waiting by the front door. "Bonjour," she greeted them. She had spent time in Alexander's shop helping the seamstresses assemble the fabrics and fix the sewing machines when they needed maintenance.

"You should all go home for the day. Alexander is not feeling well and I cannot manage the shop floor today," she partially lied. "He asked me to pick something up for him, I only need a moment but then will be locking the door again."

One of the women peered into the cab curiously while Elsa was in the shop. When she emerged from the store a few minutes later with a second backpack, the two women appeared even more confused as the taxicab drove off.

Alfons hadn't spent much time at his father's shop on Rue Lafayette, the way he had spent time at their store in Vienna. The set-up in Paris was smaller than the production facility in Vienna, and it suddenly dawned on him to ask what would become of the business. Would it operate while his father was mobilized in the French army? Would it have to close since no one was there to run it? Would the Nazis take control of the business like they did to the business in Vienna?

**Live and Be Counted**

Other ominous questions ran through his mind. What if the Nazis discovered his father in a French military uniform? Would they recognize him as the Austrian that deceived Eichmann and Huber and managed to escape Vienna from under their nefarious eyes? Would they take him prisoner or, even worse, kill him? How would his father defend himself if he wasn't armed?

The taxicab brought the four wayfarers to an area about ten kilometers outside of the city with several warehouses and stables. Helena was familiar with the layout since she often accompanied her husband on his distribution routes, and even on a few occasions managed the route herself when he was ill and unable to work. She directed the driver to the stable where her husband's horse was kept. When it stopped, they all came out of the vehicle and Elsa paid the driver with Francs from her backpack.

Helena guided the horse from the stable to the warehouse and attached the harness to the carriage tow. Helena, Alfons and Elsa secured a small canopy to the carriage that was used to keep Helena's husband dry on rainy days. The canopy looked tattered and torn and Alfons hoped it was in good enough condition to keep them dry from rain and equally shaded from the sun. It was becoming increasingly warmer with each spring day that came.

The carriage was more like a loading haul. There was a front bench for the driver, which could sit two people, and Helena motioned to Alfons to sit up front with her. "I'm going to teach you how to drive a horse and carriage so you can take control of the reigns when I need to rest." Elsa and Helgi sat on two milk crates in the back of the carriage surrounded their luggage.

Helena steered the horse from the warehouse area and eventually reached Highway A10, which was the main road leading out of Paris. After the city receded to the likes of a painted background, Alfons looked ahead and saw endless rows of grassy fields with wheat and cornstalks waving peacefully in the morning

## Chapter 13

wind. He was used to the hustling and noises that came along with living in a densely populated city.

Vineyards and wineries dotted the sides of the road. Occasionally, they passed worn cottages and red barns that stood lonesome in the pastures and Alfons wondered whether anyone lived in them or took care of the surrounding land. The scenery reminded him of the Sunday countryside drives that he took with his mother and father in Vienna. Alfons looked up to his left and Helena flashed him a smile. "He's a young, strong horse and maybe one day he will race in the Hippodrome in Deauville," she laughed at the silliness of the thought and Alfons smiled back.

"*Merci de nous avoir accompagné*, Madame Bensimon," Alfons said in perfect French. Thank you for giving us a ride.

"*Vous êtes les bienvenus, jeune homme*," Helena responded. "*Nous aurons beaucoup de temps pour parler français.*" We will have plenty of time to practice your French along the way.

Elsa never really heard Alfons talk in French. She herself had picked up very few words in the nearly two years they were living in France and only spoke German to him at home. She admitted being surprised, actually impressed at how well her son appeared to have picked up the language.

It was a two-day journey by horse, Helena said, and they would need to find a place to sleep overnight. They rode continuously for nearly ten hours, stopping just a few times to water the horse with rain-filled troughs on the side of the road. The sun beat down on them throughout the day, and for a few moments at a time when the sun hid behind a set of moving clouds, they could feel relief under the weathered canopy. Alfons tried to excite his sister whenever they passed a herd of cows or hogs, launching a parade of animal sounds that Helgi tried to mimic.

## Live and Be Counted

They ate and drank sparingly from the limited food and canteens that they had brought. Occasionally, Helena let Alfons steer the horse, and when he did, he pretended to be an American cowboy from the cinema pulling the reigns up and down to pick up the speed.

With the sun beginning to make its descent over France, Elsa suggested that they find a place to sleep. Helgi had been as good as could be expected, but it wasn't realistic that they could travel through the night. They came to a roadside cottage and Alfons could faintly see lines of vineyards draping the land. He assumed the structure beyond the cottage was a pressing facility to turn the grapes into wine.

Helena brought the horse to a stop and Elsa jumped out of the carriage. She approached a middle-aged man who was tending to a small garden with his wife on the side of his house. "*Bonjour*, we just need a place to sleep for the night," she begged the farmer. "We are four people, including one very young child. I will pay you for your troubles."

The farmer peered into the carriage, seeing the other woman and the two children. "*Etes-vous Juif?*" the farmer asked to no one in particular.

"*Oui*," Alfons answered. "Yes, we are Jewish. *Nous sommes Français, comme vous.* And we are French, just like you," he added trying to make an appeal.

Elsa pulled several Franc notes from her bag and extended her hand to the farmer. Alfons watched her motions and noticed that she did not even look to count the amount she was giving him. The farmer took the Francs without hesitation and pointed to the red barn to the right of the house in the distance, indicating where they could sleep for the night. "*Ils peuvent y domir.*"

## Chapter 13

"*Merci*," Helena and Elsa both thanked the farmer in unison.

Alfons, Elsa, Helgi and Helena climbed from the carriage, hauling their bags, and followed the farmer to the red barn. The farmer opened the door and pulled on a long string hanging from a lightbulb at the top of the barn which illuminated the space. The sudden brightness startled some of the sleeping cows. A group of mosquitos and flies that were spread throughout the barn collected around the light source high above them. The air felt thick and filled their noses with the pungent odor of manure.

Unaccustomed to nighttime visitors, the farmer's wife heard voices outside and joined her husband at the entrance of the barn. The farmer mumbled to his wife in French, but it was inaudible and Alfons could not make out what he was saying. He could sense that the farmer's wife was not happy about the sleeping arrangement for which he had accepted payment. The farmer avoided eye contact with the four Jewish vagabonds standing helplessly in his barn. He turned his back and headed back to the cottage.

The farmer's wife seemed to linger just a bit longer, staring pitifully at the four of them, which sent a wave of fear and a dose of reality shivering down Alfons' spine. Unexpectedly, she chillingly offered a warning. "The Germans are ruthless. No matter where your hiding spot, they will find you and send you to prison. May God have mercy on your souls." She closed the barn doors as she returned to the cottage, leaving Elsa, Helena, Alfons and Helgi alone with a long night to reflect on their journey and the vast unknown that still lay ahead.

They looked around and found a stack of hay in between the stables toward the back of the barn. "Mother," Alfons tried to lighten the situation, "it's just like the hotel we stayed at in

Altenmartk when we used to go skiing in Austria. Only this has taller ceilings!"

Elsa paused at the absurdity of Alfons' statement, and then erupted in laughter, causing Alfons to laugh too. They laughed at the sadness of the situation and how far they were from their comfortable lives in Vienna. Their apartment, their car, their business and community, all which had been lost to them. The Altenmartk memory made Alfons think of his father. They were two hundred kilometers away from him, assuming he was still in Paris, and that was a large, unfounded assumption.

Helgi cried of hunger and Elsa tried to have her nibble on whatever was left from the crust of the sandwiches she had made for the first leg of the journey. Alfons was hungry too, but kept it to himself hoping that his strength would be back in the morning. He was more worried about the horse flies and mosquitos he saw earlier by the light and imagined swarms of them flying overhead, preparing their attack on his raw skin. Alfons covered himself and Helgi with rain jacket from their bags, dually serving to keep warm at night and protected from the biting insects. Eventually, they all curled themselves into a deep sleep of exhaustion and hunger.

# Chapter 14

May 8, 2020

"Good afternoon Eli, how was school today?" Papa asked.

"Hi Papa!" Eli responded. "It was great. We learned about something different other than the usual math and science. Did you know that today is the seventy-fifth anniversary of the end of World War Two?"

Alfons had been reading the New York Times earlier that morning and was captured by the significance of the anniversary. His readership of the New York Times dated back more than fifty years to the 1960s when he would purchase a copy on his way to work for twenty cents. Now, he had home delivery for about one dollar per day and accessed its content online.

Papa knew that the war had waged on between the US and Japan for a few more months, but the United States and England declared victory in Europe when Germany surrendered on May 8, 1945, exactly seventy-five years ago.

"It's amazing to think that some people who fought and lived through the war are still alive today," Eli considered. "How did Germany come to surrender if they had gained so much control of Europe?"

"The United States, England, Canada and few smaller countries joined to strategize ways of defeating Nazi Germany, becoming known as the Allied Forces. Ultimately, they coordinated plans to mount the largest amphibious invasion the world had ever known."

## Live and Be Counted

"A what type of invasion?" Eli interrupted. *Amphibian* was a word he never heard before.

"Have you ever heard of an amphibian animal?" Papa redirected.

"Maybe, I think so," Eli stuttered, buying himself some time as he quickly switched his screen from Zoom to Google to search on the word. "Papa how do you spell amphibian? A. M. F."

"No, there is no F. It's A. M. P. H. I."

"I got it!" Eli said excitedly as the word auto-filled in the Google search bar and he clicked on the term to reveal its definition. "It says that an amphibian is a type of animal that is born in the water but can also live on land. So you mean the invasion of the Allied Forces started in the sea and moved to land, like a frog?"

Papa confirmed. "In June 1944, the Allied Forces had over one hundred and fifty thousand soldiers mount a seaborne attack against the Germans, coming across the English Channel and landing on the beaches of Normandy, France where the Germans had put up defensive barriers. The Germans had been controlling France, Holland, Belgium and Luxemburg for more than four years at this point."

"Many soldiers from the Allied Forces lost their lives in the first few days of the battle at Normandy," Papa continued. "Overall, they were successful in pushing the German soldiers back and taking control of France's northern coast. Battleships and navy sea carriers remained in the Channel and provided ongoing supplies to the soldiers like food, first aid and clothing. The ships also paved a crucial gateway to bring more troops to Normandy. The Normandy invasion was the first military battle that ultimately led to the liberation of Europe from Germany."

## Chapter 14

"What happened to all the soldiers that died in the battle of Normandy? Did they get brought back to America?" Eli asked.

"Actually, there is now a cemetery in Normandy on a cliff overlooking the English Channel that has almost ten thousand graves of soldiers who were killed during battle. Most of them were Christian and their plots are marked by marble white crosses with their name, rank, and dates of birth and death etched into the stone. There are also about one hundred and fifty Jewish stars embedded throughout the cemetery for the American Jewish soldiers who were killed in the battle. If you look online, I'm sure you can find pictures."

Eli was on the Google page that produced the definition of *amphibian* and he navigated back to the search bar to type *Normandy Cemetery Pictures*. His page loaded with scores of pictures, some color and some black and white, of the most perfect, symmetrically organized rows of white gravestones. Eli thought that the grave markers rose courageously through the perfectly manicured green grass. He zoomed in on a few pictures and, sure enough, spotted several Jewish stars amongst the endless rows of crosses.

"The US government wasn't able to bring the fallen soldiers back home?" Eli wondered why they were buried in France and not in the United States closer to their families.

"The bodies of many soldiers killed by German snipers positioned at the top of the cliff were never recovered and remained at the bottom of the English Channel. Most families felt it would be honorable for their soldiers to be buried in the place alongside comrades with whom they died fighting."

Eli was still scrolling through other pictures that came up in his *Normandy* search. There was one picture showing hundreds of vessels in the water that captured his attention, capturing. The

**Live and Be Counted**

view was from the top of one of the cliffs overlooking the beach and must have been taken after the Allied Forces had gained control of the area following the invasion. The picture liberated Eli's imagination of what it must have been like to storm across the channel in a battleship and swim to the shores wearing a uniform and carrying a gun. In the picture, he noticed a metal bridge in the water supporting with a tank.

"Wow," he reacted in amazement. "They brought tanks onto the ships and then built interlocking bridges to connect them to the land. Now I see what you mean about this being the largest ampi… amfib…"

"Amphibious," Papa helped him out.

"Right," Eli picked up where he left off. "Amphibious invasion in the history of the world. What happened after Normandy? Did the Nazis surrender?"

"Not quite yet," Papa answered. "At that point during the Holocaust, I was hiding in Switzerland and news spread pretty quickly that the Allied Forces were on the offensive. With the Americans involved in the war, optimism was very high that the Germans would be defeated. Reports at the time were mixed with rumors and getting accurate information on what was really happening was difficult. A lot of what I know today was learned much later after the war when accounts were published in various books and produced through movies. Grandma Phyllis and I actually traveled to Normandy about ten years ago to see the museums and visit the military cemeteries."

Eli was getting lost in the story again. "How did you end up in Switzerland? Weren't you living in France when the German's came in?"

## Chapter 14

"Let's put Switzerland to the side for the time being. A lot happened before that I want to tell you about. Let's go back to the Allied Forces landing in Normandy."

"OK," Eli went back to reimagining himself as a soldier swimming through the waters. Papa mentioned that the Normandy invasion happened in June, so Eli hoped that the waters were warm and not too frigid for the soldiers.

"Over the next nine months, the Allied Forces gradually pushed the Germans back, battle by battle, through the cities of Normandy, finally defeating them in Paris and taking back the capital of France. French fighters, who had retreated to the south of France and formed their own resistance, joined the Allied Forces to help liberate France in August of 1944."

Alfons recounted how over the coming months, US, Canadian and British forces continued their push into Germany. The Allied Forces were shocked at the massive number of corpses and rail-thin bodies of people barely hanging to life when they liberated camps like Dachau, Auschwitz and Bergen-Belsen in April of 1945. Unfortunately, thousands of Jews continued to die from starvation and disease, even after the camps were liberated.

"When it became clear that the Allied Forces were overpowering the Germans and liberating the camps, Adolf Hitler committed suicide by swallowing a cyanide pill on April 30, 1945. The Germans unconditionally surrendered a week later on May 8, 1945."

Eli calculated that most of soldiers who fought in World War Two and still alive at the seventy-fifth anniversary must be in their late nineties. Instead of military parades to honor the soldiers, living veterans around the world were encouraged to hang a flag from their window and observe a moment of silence in unison. Many did so alone, without family and without comrades with whom they had served.

There was a pause in the conversation, as each of them seemed to internalize the enormous significance of the day, the classic victory of good over evil, the return of inalienable freedoms and dignities that were stripped from millions of people.

In reality, Alfons knew that for many, including his own family, life did not return to normal. Countries that got swept into the war, whether by choice or by conquest, saw their cities, homes and businesses reduced to rubble after six years of fighting. For the next forty-five years, some of the Eastern European countries like Poland, Romania, Czechoslovakia and Hungary came under the control of Russia. For the Jews that had survived the Holocaust, there was no home, no life, which to return.

"I hear my parents talk about the economy, with so many people losing their jobs as the government tries to keep people at home to stop the spread of the virus," Eli said. "You told me that Hitler emerged to power because so many people were hopeless and did not have jobs. Do you think that can happen again?"

"I sure hope not," Papa considered his response and thought to himself how the coronavirus was wreaking economic turmoil, leaving people without jobs and creating desperation. It was not farfetched to envision how desperation could bring out the worst in people.

"I sure hope not," he said again.

# Chapter 15

Mid May 1940

Sleep seemed like a fleeting, unsatisfied moment when the farmer opened the rustic doors at the crack of dawn, allowing the rising sun to illuminate the inside of the barn. His movement set off a cacophony of animal-sounding instruments of *moos* and *nehs* that made Helgi giggle. "At least she's happy this morning," Alfons said stretching his arms, still feeling tired from a restless night.

The farmer was carrying a bag and jug in his hands. "I've brought you some biscuits and milk," he said extending the food to them. "Please eat quickly, you need to leave right away. The newspapers are reporting that the war with Germany is going to escalate and we cannot take the risk of hiding Jews. Now please, get your carriage hitched to the horse and be on your way."

Alfons, Elsa, Helgi and Helena were so hungry that they shoveled the breakfast into their mouths without typical regard for etiquette. They gathered their belongings and climbed back into the carriage with their bags, thanking the farmer and his wife who both bade them well.

Helena steered the horse back to the main road and the hoofs created a clopping rhythm that induced Alfons to get lost in his own thoughts. It seemed that the sentiment toward Jews was one of inner conflict, and perhaps many Frenchmen were uncertain exactly how to feel, worried about how others would feel toward them.

The Nazi influence of Jewish hatred was palpable, for sure, and the French were going to protect their own before they protected others. Alfons thought about his father again. It had been several weeks since his enlistment into the French Civil Corps and he imagined him in his French uniform proudly serving adjacent to other Frenchmen. People like his father would convince the others that Jews who fled to France from other countries were worthy of living here, just like the native French.

As they rode mostly in silence for several uneventful hours, Alfons noticed that they were not alone. He looked ahead of them and behind them, seeing a large convoy of travelers moving in the same direction as they were. Every so often, an automobile filled to the limit of its physical capacity, tried to navigate the same road through the horse-drawn carriages, sounding their horn impatiently to get ahead on Highway A10.

Thousands of Jews had formed a caravan of carriages and cars leaving Paris.

Several times they stopped to buy fruit and drink water at roadside stands, and there were other horse and carriages, as well as occasional cars. Alfons even recognized some of the teenagers from his neighborhood and school. It suddenly occurred to him that there must have been hundreds, perhaps thousands, of Jews fleeing toward Bordeaux.

The gentle air was warm with the sun shining overhead and the carriage provided shade from the rays as the morning hit high noon. Around midday, they stopped at a roadside produce stand where his mother bought apples for Alfons and Helgi. Alfons overheard the chatter of several others standing near the produce stand that sent pulsating waves of dread through his body.

"The German soldiers have invaded France from the north and are on their way to Paris."

"The French government is going to surrender."

## Chapter 15

"I heard many French soldiers have already been taken as prisoners of war."

Alfons could not direct his fear-wrought thoughts away from the image of his father in uniform with his hands tied behind his back being marched to a prisoner camp by the Germans. He stared up at the sky, his eyes nearly blinded by the strength of the sun above, appealing mercifully to the God he wanted so much to believe in. The God his father believed in. The God that had kept them safe and one step ahead of Nazis all this time.

His mind penetrated the inner depths of his soul where he kept a healthy reserve of faith that, from time to time, needed to be called upon. Alfons began to recite under his breath a short prayer from Psalms that he said in school whenever someone was sick or in trouble and needed God's help. He needed that for his father now and begged God to keep him safe.

With his eyes still squinting upward toward the brilliant sun, Alfons didn't notice the scattering of birds or hear the swooshing sound of the propellers. He suddenly felt his knees and palms scrape the gravel beneath with painful intensity. He became momentarily disoriented as his mother suddenly and forcefully pushed him down to the ground.

*Tatatatatatata*.

Alfons thought the clopping of the horse's hooves was unusual, growing louder and faster with each passing moment.

*Tatatatatatata*.

Could those repetitive sounds be coming from the hoofs of the horses, he thought? It couldn't be since the horses were stationary and they were standing on the side of the road.

*Tatatatatatata*.

## Live and Be Counted

Suddenly, he saw their horse lean back against its hind legs and raise its front hoofs into the sky, crying out loudly in primal fear.

*Tatatatatatata.*

At that instant, Alfons realized the repetitive sound was coming from up above. He looked up and saw planes thundering in the sky. German planes. He could see small plumes of dirt jump up from the earth in linear patterns.

"Stay down!" his mother yelled, "Just stay down!"

Helgi had been sitting on the ground eating the apple slices when the bullets began zipping by. Instinctively, Alfons pulled Helgi under his chest and created a human shield, as he crawled with her, his mother and Helena underneath the cart that was hooked to the horse.

The cart in which they had been riding for the last two days was now sheltering them from the onslaught of machine gun fire by the German Luftwaffe flying overhead. Helena was shaking, lying on the ground next to Elsa. Elsa draped her arm around Alfons, while Alfons buried Helgi in his chest, ready to protect her if a bullet found them lying under the cart.

They laid motionless underneath the cart for what felt like an eternity, only their labored, panicked breathing breaking the silence. Even Helgi, who was just two years old, seemed to comprehend the gravity of the moment and held her silence. Alfons held Helgi's head in his palm, protecting it against the ground as he lay on top of her under the cart. Eventually, the drone of the fighter planes faded inaudibly into the distance until they could no longer be heard or seen.

Helena, Elsa, Alfons and Helgi continued to be still, praying that Luftwaffe was not returning. Suddenly, shattering the stillness

## Chapter 15

that had overtaken the scene, a woman nearby cried out an awful scream, the likes of which Alfons had never heard, sending tremors of fear down his spine. Alfons lifted his head from under the carriage and recognized the screaming from a woman who had been standing near them at the fruit stand. She was kneeling beside one of the men that Alfons had overheard discussing Germany's invasion of France before the warplanes roared overhead.

Alfons could see the man grabbing his leg from an apparent bullet wound while blood was oozing through his pants. Alfons began to feel dizzy and pulled himself into a seated position on the ground to prevent himself from passing out from the sight of the blood.

Elsa also crawled out from underneath the cart and pulled herself up, brushing off the dirt and pebbles that clung to her shirt and legs. She ran over to the bleeding man and tried to inspect the wound, but she had no medical training did not know how to dislodge the bullet or stop the bleeding.

Alfons regained his composure through a rush of adrenaline and ran to his mother's side next to the wounded man. He remembered a scene from an American cowboy movie where the outlaw ripped his shirt off and tied it tightly around a bullet he had taken to the arm.

Elsa and Alfons stayed with the man and his wife, helping them climb back to their own horse and carriage when the man had the strength and courage to be pulled up from the ground. There was not much more they could do, except hope the couple would find a hospital where they could treat the wound.

Elsa ran back to Helena, who was still laying beneath the carriage with Helgi. "We must keep going," she said unnervingly, lifting Helgi back into the cart and extending her arm toward Alfons, motioning him to follow.

Alfons saw the fear in his mother's eyes and knew he needed to be strong. Helena was similarly trembling as she crawled out from under the carriage and pulled herself into the seat, so Alfons took hold of the reign and guided the horse back onto the road.

Eventually, the rhythmic beat of the horse's hoofs overtook the sound of their heavy breathing and they rode mostly in silence until highway signs appeared more frequent as they approached Bordeaux. The sun made its final descent over the western horizon, creating a brilliant splash of red, blue and purplish colors across the dimming sky. Helena remarked that the colors in the sky were produced by the sun setting over the great Atlantic Ocean.

Having grown up in landlocked Austria, the road to Bordeaux was as close as Alfons had ever been to an ocean, which created a bit of intrigue for him. He remembered spending hot summer days at Seewinkel National Park and going swimming in Lake Neusiedl, about an hour from their Vienna home.

The thought of being so close to the Atlantic Ocean made him think about the people on the other side of it. What was America doing while Europe was at war? Did they know about the atrocities the Nazis were committing? Did they know about the random arrests and murdering of Jews? Did they know about German warplanes shooting indiscriminately at innocent, unarmed women and children?

The horse's pace slowed as they came into the city of Bordeaux and narrow streets became congested with other horse-drawn carriages. As it became darker, streetlamps dimly lit the cobblestone roads. Helena, who had taken back the reigns from

## Chapter 15

Alfons, steered the horse through the city's Jewish Quarter toward the apartment complex where her son's family lived.

Traveling on Rue Labirat, Alfons looked to his right and was awestruck by a large white building with two symmetrical towers situated at the flanks of the central section. To him, the large towers of the building strongly evoked the bell towers of the Notre Dame Cathedral in Paris that he had visited with his class. The central section also served as the main entrance with three arched doorways and a series of vertical stained-glass windows reaching toward the top of the facade. Alfons' eyes looked upward and noticed a prominent Star of David extruding from the stone architecture. Just above the star, an impressive cornice of the Two Tablets of Moses dominated the facade at its highest point.

His eyes scanned back down the facade and, in the three main doorways, Alfons saw hundreds of people lined up in single file from the inside that extended outside onto the promenade and around the corner of the synagogue.

"This is the Great Synagogue of Bordeaux," Helena explained. "It was built in 1882 after a fire destroyed the main synagogue in 1873, which had originally stood since 1812. The Great Synagogue has over 1,500 seats, the largest in all of France."

"Why are so many people lined up to enter the synagogue?" Alfons asked.

Helena responded, "Most of these people are fleeing from cities up north like Paris, fearing the German occupation."

She turned back to Elsa and continued, "My son's apartment is small and his family barely has enough room to take me in. I'm afraid you will need to sleep at the synagogue until you find yourselves something more permanent."

### Live and Be Counted

The horse came to a gradual stop just beyond the Great Synagogue, where Elsa, Alfons and Helgi stepped down from the cart and bid their farewells to Helena. With their bags in hand, they shuffled to the end of the line and waited to be registered by men who represented the Jewish Council of Bordeaux. Alfons was hungry and Helgi was restless, his mother did her best to indulge their patience until they were registered and admitted into the synagogue.

They were ushered down a stairwell by a man in his late sixties into a great hall that laid beneath the main sanctuary. The right side of the hall was set up with tables holding pots of vegetable soup and plates of bread. On the left side of the hall were hundreds of cots lined up in several horizontal rows. Children and adults of all ages sat on their cots, some sipping soup, others unfolding clothing and removing personal items from their bags. There was a low din across the room, inaudible voices from hundreds of refugees who appeared just as tired as the Sperbers.

The man who had shown them to the main hall sported a salt and pepper beard and a white shirt that was showing its wear. "My name is Josef Cohen," he introduced himself. "I'm the rabbi at the Great Synagogue. It's a pleasure to meet you. What's your name?"

"My name is Alfons. Thank you for letting us stay here."

"Please, help yourself to food and get comfortable for the night. You look old enough to be a *Bar Mitzvah*, is that right?"

"Yes sir," Alfons answered with a hint of pride, "I became a *Bar Mitzvah* a few months ago in March living in Paris."

"Have you brought your *t'fillin* with you, young man?" he asked Alfons.

## Chapter 15

Alfons reached into his backpack and navigated his hand to the bottom where he caressed the velvet pouch that contained the leather boxes and straps he had adorned each morning on his right arm and around his head since celebrating his *Bar Mitzvah*. It was a religious imperative for every boy turning thirteen to wear the *t'fillin* each day other than Shabbat or major holidays. He nodded to the elderly man, but it distressfully occurred to him that he had not wrapped his arms and forehead with the *t'fillin* the morning after their night sleeping in the barn on the way to Bordeaux.

"Our morning services start at eight o'clock, I hope to see you there," the bearded man beseeched. "The lights will go out in about an hour, so be sure to eat up and prepare yourselves for bed. I know you had a long journey to get here."

Alfons offered to take Helgi to the food line while his mother scoped out a pod of cots where they would sleep for the night. Soup and bread were a meager dinner, but Alfons was appreciative of whatever he received. He savored the soup with small spoonfuls and modest bites of bread to make dinner last. In a vast, open room there was very little privacy and even fewer bathrooms. Alfons saw puddles of urine throughout the room from children who could not afford to wait on growing lines to use the toilets. After changing into sleepwear and helping Helgi do the same, he laid down on the cot using the thin sheet as a cover and tucked Helgi into his arms.

It hardly mattered that he was sleeping in a hall with several hundred people. Alfons' mind replayed over and over the German Luftwaffe planes firing at them from the air. He replayed the sequence of dirt erupting from the ground as it took rounds of bullets. He saw the woman from the fruit stand kneeling over her husband whose leg was struck by a bullet. He absorbed his mother's pride when he stopped the bleeding using his rain jacket as a tourniquet. He wondered if the man had survived.

Alfons replayed the scene over and over, unable to shake the whoosh of the warplane propellers or the rhythmic sounds of bullets hitting the ground. Eventually, exhaustion won the battle for his mind and he fell into a restless sleep that left him equally exhausted when children sleeping around him began awakening to the early rays of light piercing through the windows in the hall.

Alfons tried to ignore the indecipherable chatter and force himself back to sleep, but it seems only moments later that Rabbi Cohen tapped him on the shoulder and told him that morning prayers would be starting in fifteen minutes. Feeling the responsibilities of being *Bar Mitzvah*, Alfons sat up on the cot and gathered his clothes worn the prior day. He dressed quickly under the blanket as privacy was scarce and retrieved his *t'fillin* from his bag. He climbed up the flight of stairs to the main sanctuary where morning services were taking place.

He entered the hall through tall glass doors and was immediately struck by the vastness of the room. He surmised that there must have been more than one thousand seats in the sanctuary. "I guess this is why it's called the Great Synagogue," he thought to himself.

His eyes gazed forward toward the Holy Ark which housed the *Torah* scrolls. The Ark was constructed between two bronze columns and the ornamentation on the doors included twelve colored stones symbolizing the twelve tribes of Israel. A man donning a *talit* prayer shawl was chanting portions of the service from the *bimah*, an elevated platform in the center of the sanctuary which displayed a seven-branch *menorah*.

There were close to one hundred men participating in the service. "I suppose telling me I would be number ten was the

## Chapter 15

rabbi's way of cajoling me out of bed this morning," Alfons snickered to himself at the crafty tactics of Rabbi Cohen. He usually went to synagogue with his father, and feeling a bit uncomfortable being there without him, Alfons took a seat in the back row and wrapped his arm and forehead with the *t'fillin* straps.

At the conclusion of the service, Rabbi Cohen approached him and said, "Alfons, tomorrow I want you to sit closer to me. For as long as you and your mother are staying here, God needs your prayers. Our people are facing difficult times and our future is unknown. Many are on the run if they haven't already been arrested or expelled from their homes. Many have been killed. Our people need faith now more than ever, and putting on the *t'fillin* each morning for prayer inspires strength for many of our people who are struggling to find God right now."

"How do we know if God is even listening?" Alfons asked. "We've run from Vienna. We've run from Paris. Why do people hate us so much? What have we done to deserve living in such fear? I don't even know if my own father is dead or alive."

"My boy," Rabbi Cohen put his arm around his shoulder, sensing the loneliness Alfons was feeling. "We do not always understand the ways of God. He has given us many blessing in life, but he also puts us through unparalleled challenges to test our faith. I believe we are going through one of the most challenging tests of faith in the history of our people. Throughout time, nations have persecuted us... the Egyptians, the Romans, the Greeks, the Spaniards, and now the Germans."

Alfons locked in with Rabbi Cohen's eyes and listened intently.

"*V'hei She'emda*," the rabbi continued, quoting the most famous passage from the Passover *Haggadah*. "In every generation, they rise to destroy us, but the Holy One delivers us to safety and freedom. In all our scriptures, God promises that one day our people will have prosperity and peace, we just have to have patience."

"And to show our faith through our prayers," Alfons finished the rabbi's thoughts.

"Yes, and to show our faith through our prayers," Rabbi Cohen echoed.

Alfons continued to look deep into Rabbi Cohen's eyes and saw his assuredness, even though he knew Rabbi Cohen was seeing the fear in his. "Alfons, I'm telling this to you, but not your mother. It would frighten her too much. Be careful who you befriend. It's obvious you're not French."

"We are Austrian," Alfons said proudly.

"Austrian, Polish, Czech and ultimately the French Jews too," Rabbi Cohen continued, his voice lowering in tone but with elevated urgency. "It doesn't matter where you are from. Germany is already in the north of the country and will come to the south when they learn that Jews fled the main cities."

"What about you?" Alfons asked the rabbi. "What will you do? Where you will go?"

"I need to stay and care for my people here. This is where I belong and this is where I will remain. Now, go get some breakfast in the hall downstairs. I will be giving a class on this week's *Torah* portion for teenagers and adults at ten o'clock, and I hope to see you there."

"You sure will," Alfons replied to Rabbi Cohen's soothing, paternal smile.

# Chapter 16

May 10, 2020

Since their last Zoom session, Eli discovered in a Google search that less than one hundred thousand of the sixteen million US veterans who served in World War Two were still alive. He did not know how many Holocaust survivors were still alive, but understood that those generations would not be around forever. He did not know anyone who was a soldier in the war, but he was proud that his great grandfather was one of the survivors.

He was still interested in Papa's story and asked him to continue where they had left off.

"We didn't stay in Bordeaux for very long, only for about a week. Food and clothing were being donated by local Jewish residents of Bordeaux, but that wouldn't last forever. It was becoming increasingly crowded as more Jewish migrants arrived from the northern cities, and as large as the Great Synagogue was, it had exceeded its capacity. It was cramped and hygiene was becoming a problem. During the day, I needed to go out and walk around for fresh air. There were families with strollers, so sometimes I took Helgi with me."

Alfons related how German soldiers were being deployed to Bordeaux, probably to fortify the coastline on the Atlantic Ocean. He mused to himself how one day he walked around the city and bumped right into a Nazi uniformed soldier as he was turning the corner.

"Normally I would have walked in the opposite direction, but I didn't see him coming," Papa admitted.

## Live and Be Counted

Eli was nervous and remembered the first time Papa had an encounter with the Nazis in Vienna at their store.

"He stopped and asked me in broken French how to walk to the harbor," Papa said. "He seemed lost and disoriented, and probably assumed I was a regular French teenager walking home or to the store."

Papa paused for a moment and smiled with a hint of precious victory. "I had a good sense of the city after a few days of exploring and new exactly which way to the harbor. So, in perfect French I said '*prend cette voie*' and pointed him in the opposite direction!"

"Good for you, Papa! I'm not sure I would have had the same courage to fool him."

"I was proud of myself too," Papa agreed, reflecting on his bold act of trickery and realizing how foolish it was probably was. "A few days later we left the Great Synagogue and traveled to Toulouse."

"What happened to all the other Jews who were there with you at the Great Synagogue in Bordeaux?"

"I'm not really sure but maybe we can research that together."

This time Papa demonstrated his Google skills and typed in 'Bordeaux' and 'World War Two' into the search bar. A few headlines appeared and he clicked on the first one and read:

*Bordeaux served as a final station for countless of Jewish refugees who fled from northern France in May and June 1940.*

"Just as we did," Papa reinforced the validity of the reported statement and continued reading with growing heartache.

## Chapter 16

*The Nazis turned the Great Synagogue into a detention center where two-thirds of the Jewish population in Bordeaux were rounded-up and deported. Toward the end of the war, the Great Synagogue was ransacked by the Nazis.*

"Do you know what happened to Rabbi Cohen?" Eli asked.

Papa continued to read the Google search result which described Rabbi Cohen's escape.

*On the night of December 17, 1940, three members of the Gestapo accused the rabbi of joining the French Resistance. The rabbi fled the synagogue through a back door to the home of a Catholic bishop where he remained hidden with him until Bordeaux was liberated in 1945.*

"I really didn't think about him much after our week in the Great Synagogue," Papa admitted and continued to read, more uplifted than the way he began.

*After the war, Jewish survivors from Bordeaux began restoration work and in 1956 the synagogue returned to its initial capacity of fifteen hundred seats. The names of the Jews from Bordeaux who were murdered during the Holocaust are inscribed on a memorial wall located in the courtyard of the synagogue.*

"The Jewish people are resilient," Papa said. "It's extraordinary to think that anyone would come back and try to rebuild."

"Papa, let's go back to your journey to Toulouse," Eli said, anxious to hear more about his great grandfather's story.

Alfons told how Father informed Mother about his business partner who would help them in Toulouse. After purchasing tickets at the train station in Bordeaux, they traveled to Toulouse by rail for three hours uneventfully.

**Live and Be Counted**

"We arrived in Toulouse at the beginning of June 1940, just a few weeks before the armistice treaty was put in place," Papa explained, "but our safety there was short-lived and put in motion a series of difficult decisions Mother would ever have to make."

"Papa, let's pick this up another time, Eli requested. "I'm being called for dinner."

"Me too," Papa chortled as he reached to shut down his iPad.

# Part Three

## Southern France

# Chapter 17

June 1940

The train from Bordeaux carrying the three Sperbers passed through an industrial area on the outskirts of Toulouse. Alfons noticed many airfields and airplane hangars, a sight he was not used to seeing in either Vienna or Paris. There were different types of airplanes that lay motionless across several runways on both sides of the tracks.

Some of the mechanical birds looked like small passenger planes with propellers on its wings, others looked like military bombers, painted in camouflage shades of green and brown. Some of the hangars were wide open exposing a few airplanes that were just steel skeletons in the early stages of their assembly. Alfons could see several welders on tall ladders and accordion lifts using power drills and screwdrivers to secure metal plates to the aircraft frame.

Just past the airfields, Helgi pinched her nose and cried out of a strange odor. Alfons smelled it too, but he couldn't quite identify it. A mix of something metallic and smoky that seeped through the seams of the windows and doors of the moving train that singed their noses.

Elsa peered out of the window and pointed to a large brick facility with several smokestacks billowing in the distance. "It's an ammunition plant," she said to Alfons. "This is where the French are producing guns and bullets for the army. The Germans have already advanced through Holland, Belgium and Luxembourg, and are fighting their way into Paris."

## Live and Be Counted

The train continued alongside the Garonne River, which Alfons noticed was unusually brown and he wondered if it was safe to go swimming or if even the fish could even survive in it. He was also struck by the pink tone of the terra-cotta bricks that seemed to be used in most of the buildings he passed on the other side of the river.

After about two hours, the train pulled into the station and Elsa, Alfons and Helgi stepped down. The central station in Toulouse was far from the ornateness of architecture and arches as the Gare du Nord in Paris. Instead, it was more simply centered on two main concourses linked at the front of the station with ticket offices, shops and cafés. Alfons carried two bags while his mother hauled a suitcase in one hand and Helgi in the other, a similar arrangement as they had done before. Elsa held her hand tight lest she wander.

They found a bank of public telephones. Elsa told Alfons to hold Helgi's hand as she unfolded a piece of paper she was keeping in the front pocket of her bag. She inserted a few franc coins into the phone and rotated the round dial with the numbers she had written on the piece of paper until it began to ring.

"Who are you calling, Mother?" Alfons inquired, curious who she knew in Toulouse.

"Your father knows a businessman in Toulouse who bought sportswear and coats from him and resold them in the southern cities. Father told us to head to Toulouse judging that it was further from the reach of the Germans if they invaded northern Fra..." She left her statement incomplete to Alfons as a man on the other end answered the phone.

Alfons listened to his mother's side of the exchange with the man on the phone. "It is Madame Sperber... Yes, we just

## Chapter 17

arrived... We have not heard from him since April... Yes, at the central station... Thank you, we will see you soon."

Elsa turned back to Alfons and Helgi and with reassuring eyes said, "He will help us. Monsieur Martin, Father's business friend, is on his way."

When Monsieur Victor Martin arrived about an hour later in his four door, silver Peugeot with red rimmed wheels, Alfons was refueled with confidence that they had arrived in a place where the Nazis could not reach them. Monsieur Martin was a portly man, wore a dark suit with black leather shoes and used a handkerchief rather frequently during the car ride to dab the beads of sweat on his forehead. They placed their bags in the trunk and tucked into the car, Alfons riding up front.

"Young man," he addressed Alfons, "it sounds like you've been on quite a journey. What do you think of Toulouse so far?"

"Well, I've only been here for a few minutes and noticed that all of the buildings are pink and the river we passed alongside the train tracks looks rather dirty."

Monsieur Martin laughed, "The Garonne River is actually very safe and filled with fish and other wildlife. The fresh water in the river is laden with sediment and clay, the same type of light-red clay used in the bricks of the buildings. The sediment rises and falls in the river depending on the strength of the current creating a brown hue."

Alfons seemed satisfied with the detailed response. "Where are we going now?" he asked.

Monsieur Martin replied, "I own a small apartment in Grenade, a community in the northern part of Toulouse. It used to belong to my parents, and when my mother died a few years ago, I moved my father into a nursing home for the elderly since he could not live safely on his own. I've left the apartment just as my parents lived in it, so it's fully furnished and ready for use. The three of you will feel comfortable in the building."

Alfons turned to his mother, "Isn't that great? And do you think I'll be able to go back to school in September?"

He saw his mother similarly dabbing her forehead with a baby cloth she had in her bag. "Just a little motion sickness from the car ride," she said. "All of this travel may be getting to me."

Alfons didn't get the answer regarding school he was looking for. Maybe his mother did not know. Elsa placed the back of her hand against her own forehead and continued to look out the window.

Monsieur Martin drove the Peugeot north for about twenty minutes through a series of residential neighborhoods all appearing peaceful and calm. They parked in front of a row house with three stories and Monsieur Martin helped them carry the bags up the flights of stairs, opening the door to an apartment midway down the hallway. Looking around the apartment, Alfons was enamored by the ornamental furniture and wondered how quickly his sister was going to create a messy trail to ruin the pristineness of the apartment.

Alfons saw his mother reach into her backpack and hand the man a thick band of franc bills from her bag. Monsieur Martin flushed and waved off the money. "The truth is, Madame Sperber, it will be good for the apartment to have some use, make sure the water doesn't become stagnant and the air doesn't get too stale. We don't know how long this war will go on. Keep the money with you and I'll settle the debt with your husband when we meet up again."

"We are forever grateful to you Monsieur Martin," Elsa said and bid him goodbye as he retreated from the apartment.

## Chapter 17

Turning to Alfons she said, "I'm going to lay down for a bit, it's been a long day. Actually, it's been a long month. Just bring me some water and watch with your sister, please. You can start by unpacking your bags."

The apartment had two bedrooms which were split by a bathroom between them on the other side of the living room wall. Elsa peeked into the first room, then the second room which she claimed as hers and laid down on the bed.

Alfons found drinking glasses in one of the kitchen cabinets and filled three of them with water from the sink. He gave one to Helgi as he sipped on his glass, and took the third one to his mother. She had already fallen asleep by the time he brought her the drink and he noticed how she was sweating from the brow. He found a washcloth in the bathroom, soaked it in warm water, and folded it gently over his mother's forehead. Alfons took some francs from his mother's bag, took Helgi by the hand and trotted down the three flights of steps together. They would need some basic groceries if this was going to be their new housing arrangement.

Alfons remembered passing a bakery and other shops on their drive through Grenade to the apartment. He traced back those steps with Helgi, patiently holding her hand so she would not wander and occasionally hoisting her atop his shoulders so they would hasten the pace.

"Can I have cookie, Al? I'll be a good girl." Helgi tugged at her brother's hand as they passed the bakery and both became swept into the store by the sweet, fresh aroma.

"Of course, Helgi," Alfons laughed at his sister's precious bargaining. "It has to be a cookie with chocolate sprinkles and you have to give your brother a bite."

## Live and Be Counted

As it turned out, the grocery store and bakery were only a few blocks away, which helped matters since he hadn't quite considered the logistics of bringing back grocery bags with a toddler taking small steps alongside him. He kept the purchases minimal to milk, bread, cereal, eggs and vegetables. He also located a kosher butcher where they could buy meat and chicken. For tonight, he would surprise his mother by preparing scrambled eggs and toast, a worthy dinner for all of them.

On the walk home, Alfons contemplated when he would be able to go to school and whether he would make new friends. He closed his hand and began releasing one finger at time. This would be his fifth school in two years.

They began their climb back up the three flights of stairs, but Helgi insisted on being carried. Alfons considered that if she did not get used to the stairwell climb now, he would be carrying her in perpetuity. He decided there would be another day to set those expectations and compassionately relented. He hauled Helgi up the stairs and returned to bring the remaining grocery bags that he left in the vestibule. Alfons placed the food on the dining room table and began his search through the drawers and cabinets for utensils and pans to prepare scrambled eggs and toast.

Alfons finished preparing dinner, but his mother did not wake and slept all the way through the night. Alfons split one of the cookies from the bakery with Helgi after they cleaned up the kitchen. He washed the pan and plates in the sink and decided that Helgi needed a bath with a good scrubbing. Eventually, he tucked her into bed wearing the lone clean pair of pajamas that his mother had packed and sang her to sleep with a lullaby.

"I want Mama to give me a kiss," Helgi stipulated as a condition for sleep, but she was already closing her eyes and giving up her negotiating leverage after a long, exhausting day.

## Chapter 17

"Mama is already sleeping, just like you'll be sleeping, too," Alfons soothed her as he finished the lullaby. "Good night, sweet Helgi. Good night."

When she was still, Alfons emerged from the bedroom and stood by the entrance to the living spaces. This apartment in Grenade, a northern neighborhood in Toulouse, would suit them just fine. There was a playground that he could see from the corner of the window and other connected row houses on the street that he figured were filled with children.

Alfons teemed with excitement to show his father their new apartment and neighborhood when he rejoined them, but reality hit him achingly back that Father was not on one of his usual business trips.

Alfons was overcome with a painful longing that Father might never rejoin them.

# Chapter 18

May 21, 2020

It had been a few weeks since Eli picked up the story with Papa. He, like many others, was settling into a home-sheltering routine as the pandemic raged on. Creative activities, videos and memes, replete with humorous cynicism over the worsening situation, spread around the Internet as quick as the virus itself, capturing whatever levity could be garnered from an economic meltdown and public health crisis that had defined the past two months. For Eli and his siblings, sleep schedules flipped upside down as the body became lethargically confused without clear delineations between virtual school and binge-watching Netflix, between round-the-clock meals and limited exercise.

Debates raged around the table and brought out spirited points of view about the origins of the coronavirus and the most effective way to deal with it. On one end, some were claiming it was manufactured in a lab for biological warfare. On the other end, some were insisting the virus was a divine intervention for families to strengthen personal relationships with each other through the quarantine time at home.

The mainstream view was that the global, interconnectedness of societies accelerated the transmission of the virus to even the most geographically isolated places. Whether the conspiracy theorists or the pragmatists were right did not matter. The effect on everyday life was undeniable.

The United States Congress responded with the largest economic stimulus package in the country's history, pumping trillions of dollars to support failing industries, small businesses

## Chapter 18

and individuals that were impacted by government orders to shut down. Restaurants and retail stores pivoted their service toward delivery and curb-side pick-up. Online retailers, touting next day delivery, showed cracks of vulnerability with pressure on manufacturing, shipping logistics and distribution. Household products like toilet paper and bread became scarce, while other products like face masks and hand sanitizers commanded premium prices.

The digital advances that defined the prior decade enabled many establishments and businesses to continue semi-normal operations through the Internet. Even Papa and Grandma Phyllis, into their nineties, had mastered the digital channel and were able to receive nearly all their groceries through online purchases and doorstep delivery. Still, they craved to go outside, to see neighbors and family, and to attend prayer services at the synagogue where they consistently attended. The rabbi of the synagogue checked in on them often by phone, but loneliness and isolation were setting in.

"Papa," Eli began to form a question that he had been thinking about for quite some time. "Did you ever think about which experience was worse? Hiding from the Nazis during the Holocaust or hiding from the coronavirus?"

"I don't think we can ever compare the genocide of six million people to anything else in modern history," Papa responded unequivocally. "When I was your age, I knew who my enemy was. They wore uniforms with swastikas and held guns. They shot bullets at us and dropped C-250 Flammbombes from the sky. They targeted us because we were Jewish. When I saw a Nazi, I knew to go the other way."

"Oh Papa, I didn't mean to suggest the pandemic and the Holocaust were the same," Eli said with a hint of regret of even suggesting they were.

## Live and Be Counted

"The coronavirus is different," Papa contemplated. "The virus isn't everywhere, but it could be anywhere. We know it isn't targeting its host based on religion or race. What is frightening about Covid is that it could lurk unknowingly in neighbors and friends, it could come from family members and it could be passed on to and from doctors. Your friends, your help, your lifelines are all potential transmitters of a deadly virus. How do you protect yourself, how do you run from an enemy that you cannot see?"

"Papa, you and Grandma Phyllis need to be extra careful, especially at your age," Eli warned. "I don't think it's worth the risk to even go outside of your house."

"It gets lonely sometimes, but the loneliness I felt eighty years ago far exceeds the loneliness we feel today. We're blessed that so many people check in on us and today's technologies bring them closer than ever before. Let's also applaud the teams of scientists who are collaborating across the world to develop a vaccine to fight off this invisible enemy," Papa continued. "The Nazis were humanity at its worst and there were many collaborators who handed Jews over to them. Back then, we were hopeless that anyone would come to our rescue."

"Papa, can we go back to your story? We left off where you, Grandma Elsa and Helgi arrived in Toulouse and were able to stay in an apartment owned by one of your father's business partners," Eli recapped.

"Soon after we arrived in Toulouse, Mother's condition worsened."

The nausea, the tiredness, the feverish sweat. Eli didn't realize that those symptoms could be Grandma Elsa becoming ill during the trip and upon their arrival in Toulouse.

## Chapter 18

"She remained in bed for the first two weeks, with a high fever and clutching her abdomen in intense pain. Monsieur Martin came to check in on us about two weeks after we arrived and, seeing Mother in the ill condition she was, drove her to the hospital."

"What was wrong with Grandma Elsa?" Eli tried to envision what a hospital would have looked like in 1940. He imagined male doctors wearing traditional dark scrubs and female nurses wearing folded caps and white coats, far different than the gender mix in today's medical field.

"She was brought to the Hôpital de La Grave that was part of the University of Toulouse where medical students trained. It was about thirty minutes from the apartment near the center of the city on the bank of the Garonne River. At the hospital, the doctors evaluated her predicament and determined that she needed an emergency hysterectomy."

Papa paused, "Eli, do you know what a hysterectomy is?"

Eli nodded his head.

"Basically," Papa knowing that Eli was only ten years old, "doctors had to remove the parts in Mother's body where babies grow before they are born. She had a bad infection that was causing internal bleeding in her uterus and ovaries which had to be removed through surgery."

"Was she able to go home after the surgery?"

"It was a difficult surgery to perform eighty years ago. Mother developed a bad infection that required her to remain under the care of doctors in the hospital for two months."

"That's a long time to be hospitalized. Did they have to put Grandma Elsa on a ventilator?" Eli asked.

## Live and Be Counted

"No, they did not put her on a ventilator, but she needed a lot of medication and time to recover from the surgery and infection. That left just me and Helgi living in the apartment, alone. Each day, we took the bus to visit Mother in the hospital. She wrote down for me simple recipes to make for dinner. Every other day, I walked to the grocery store and bought food to cook for me and Helgi."

"Papa, remind me how old you were?"

"I was thirteen and Helgi was only two."

Eli stared through the computer screen into Papa's steel-blue eyes, trying to imagine those eyes on a young, determined teenager eighty years before. He was in awe that at thirteen years old his great grandfather was taking care of his baby sister, alone in a foreign city, while his mother recovered from a serious infection and the fate of his father remained unknown.

At the same time, Alfons reflected on those two months as well, watching my baby sister by himself, feeding her, bathing her, playing with her, changing her diaper. "I was her only parent until Mother was well enough to be released from the hospital."

"That is a lot to ask of any thirteen-year-old," Eli said in awe, wondering if he would have been able to take on those responsibilities himself.

Alfons never considered it a burden, recognizing the predicament they were in and doing what was needed to survive. He thought serenely about his sister Helgi, her own children she had raised and the grandchildren and great grandchildren that were blessed to her. The care Alfons showed for Helgi eighty years ago still appeared today, calling her daily during the pandemic.

"We were happy to have Mother back, for sure," Papa answered. "I was able to enroll in eighth grade at the local school

## Chapter 18

in September, even though my education had been so disrupted for the last two years since fleeing Vienna. My French had become more fluent, but I was still marked as an outsider, which was even more pronounced in a city like Toulouse than it was in Paris. Mother implored me to just go to school, come home and do my homework. She did not want me to become too comfortable or invest in deep friendships."

Papa told Eli how Toulouse began to suffer deprivation and food shortages in 1941, the effects of supply chains being cut off and diverted to the Germans in the north. Mother took a job as a seamstress and sent Helgi to a nursery while she worked.

"We began to notice Germans soldiers patrolling parts of the city," Papa said ominously. "We became increasingly frightened about staying in Toulouse and reports were circulating about detention centers for Jews in the south. It was rumored that some French were collaborating with the Germans to identify Jews who had fled from the north."

Papa continued, "Thankfully though, not everyone was against us. There was an archbishop in Toulouse named Jules-Gérard Saliège who was a vigorous critic of the French authorities that were collaborating with the Germans. In November 1941, he published a letter questioning why the French Catholic hierarchy did not do more to provide protection and sanctuary for Jews who were being targeted for detention and deportation by the Nazis. The letter was circulated by members of the French Resistance throughout the country and emboldened clergymen and nuns to hide Jewish children."

"Papa, how did you know about the archbishop?" Eli asked.

"When I traveled to Israel for the first time in 1985, I visited *Yad Vashem*, the national Holocaust Memorial Museum in Jerusalem. I tried to learn about the places where I lived during the war and discovered that the museum had recognized Archbishop Jules-Gérard Saliège as *Righteous Among the Nations* for his actions to hide Jewish children during the war amid personal risks."

"He wasn't the only person from Toulouse who was recognized as 'Righteous Among the Nations' by *Yad Vashem*," Papa reflected. "In 1941, Alice Resch Synnestvedt played a critical role in saving my life, as well as the life of my sister Helgi."

"To me, Alice was the most righteous of them all."

## Chapter 19

August 1940 – March 1941

Elsa returned from the hospital in August 1940, declared by the medical staff healthy and free of infection. The doctors and nurses who treated her did so without regard to her religious faith or nationality. "They took care of me as a member of the human race," Elsa related to the neighbors who greeted her with fruit baskets, fresh bread and other sweets. When they heard that the mother of the two children who had been living on their own was ready to make her triumphant return, the women welcomed her at the entrance to the apartment building.

"It's our pleasure to meet you," a woman with a six-year-old girl and a four-year old boy introduced herself as Leah Weiss and extended her hand to Elsa. "We've come from Germany, as did Miriam Kaiser and Hannah Schechter," who were also surrounded by children and shared their smiles with Elsa. The four women formed an immediate bond shared by common origins and flights.

Alfons enrolled in eighth grade at the Toulouse public school in September 1940 and Elsa brought Helgi to a two-year old nursery, while she worked part-time as a seamstress. With each passing month, however, Alfons noticed an increase presence of German soldiers patrolling around Toulouse. At first, the Nazis appeared casual, drinking coffee at cafes and smoking cigarettes in small groups at street corners. As their presence grew, Alfons also sensed a palpable distancing of his peers in school. The growing isolation was reminiscent of the days at the Gymnasium in Vienna shortly after *Anschluss*.

### Live and Be Counted

Monsieur Martin occasionally checked in on Elsa and the children, and she confided in him her trepidation that the Nazi patrols were alarming the Jews, especially immigrant Jews as herself. "Don't worry too much, Madame Sperber," Monsieur Martin tried his best to reassure her. "We are governed by the French in the south. German soldiers have been stationed here to dissuade any resistance that could emerge and threaten the occupation. The Jews in Toulouse will be safe as long as you don't give the Nazis any reason to suspect you might cause them trouble."

One Saturday in December 1940, Elsa and the children walked to Leah Weiss' apartment, as they often did for *Shabbat* dessert and tea. They knocked on the door, but there was no answer. Unperturbed, Elsa figured Leah had gone out and suggested they walk to Hannah Schechter's apartment which was around the corner.

"Have you not heard, Elsa?" Hannah cautioned, grabbing her arm and pulling Elsa into the apartment with Alfons and Helgi following. "No one has seen Leah or the children in almost a week. It's as if they've disappeared."

"Are you thinking what I'm thinking?" Elsa asked Hannah hesitantly, also weary that Alfons was listening behind her. "Do you think they were arrested?"

"How can we know?" Hannah admitted. "There are more and more Nazis patrolling the streets each day. There are rumors that the French are acting as informants, letting the Nazis know where Jews are living. Not the French Jews, but the Jews who came from Germany and Austria, like you and me."

## Chapter 19

Elsa, Hannah and Miriam stayed in close contact over the coming months, remaining vigilant of their surroundings and activities to avoid raising any suspicions.

"Have you noticed the shelves in grocery stores don't have as much food or produce anymore?" Elsa asked the other two women as they were playing cards on *Shabbat* afternoon.

"There are more people living in Toulouse now," Hannah said. "The population has swelled from all the people fleeing the occupation in the north," Hannah said.

"Food is in short supply since the Nazis are sending produce from the French farmers to the German soldiers," Miriam added. "The food that used to be delivered to our grocers are being redirected away from Toulouse."

"I'm getting very nervous," Elsa said vulnerably. "Alfons said one of his Jewish classmates hasn't been in school all week."

One Saturday afternoon in March, at their standing time for dessert and tea, Elsa was rattled by a panicked knocking at the door. She hurried to the front of the apartment, but held back and cautiously peered through the eyehole. She was relieved when she recognized Hannah on the other side and opened the door to watch Hannah stumble into the apartment short of breath.

"It's Miriam!" she cried. "They've arrested her. The Nazis arrested her! I saw them marching her in the street with the children. Elsa, what are we going to do?"

For the next several hours, the women comforted each other in the apartment and talked through their possibilities. They did not know where to go, and it was becoming too perilous to stay where they were. Alfons listened closely, solemn over the helplessness they were feeling again and scared that the next knock could be the Nazis with an arrest warrant.

## Live and Be Counted

That week, Elsa called Monsieur Martin for guidance. "Toulouse is too dangerous, first Leah and now Miriam. It's too dangerous for us to remain here. I'm no different than those two women. Unwelcome immigrants in the French eyes, unwanted Jews in the Nazi eyes. We will be marked for arrest, like the others."

"Elsa, there is a Quaker woman I heard who has been secretly helping Jews hide their children," Monsieur Martin said. "Go find her, maybe she can help you. Whatever you decide, you can continue to stay in the apartment." He gave Elsa an address and bid her luck and farewell.

Elsa was scared and desperate, arriving at the Quaker office with her two children later that week. A woman in her young thirties, wearing a spring dress to welcome the warming temperatures, answered the door. She saw the pitiful look in the woman's eyes standing before her and, without even a word being exchanged, immediately knew why she had come.

"Good afternoon, Madame. My name is Elsa Sperber," Elsa introduced herself with growing trepidation. She was questioning if she had come to the right place and perhaps if she should have come at all. "I have heard secretly that you help people. People like me. Jewish people, that is."

"Good afternoon, Madam Sperber. My name is Alice Resch," she replied looking into the fretful eyes of the woman and two children standing with her. She looked beyond Elsa and wondered if her husband, like other Jewish men, had been killed or taken prisoner. Without asking, Alice knew that a heavy request was about to be made, but she did not know if she could save the two children in front of her.

Born in 1908, Alice Resch spent her formative youth growing up in Norway and was inspired to become a nurse after

## Chapter 19

visiting the pediatric ward of the American Hospital in Paris as a teenager. In 1940, Alice joined the American Friends Service Committee, which had established itself as a nongovernmental organization of the Quakers, rooted in Christian faith and powered by the belief that each person has a unique worth. Through the AFSC, she channeled her efforts to help children displaced by the mounting conflict and placed them in foster homes, orphanages and medical facilities.

Over the last year, Alice watched waves of Jewish transplants arrive in Toulouse from northern France following the German occupation. More recently, she was hearing about increased deportations of Jews by French Police acting on behalf of the Nazis who were charged with arresting those who had fled from the north. Many of those arrested were being interred under Nazi-controlled detention camps us as Saint-Sulpice-la-Pointe and Recebedou near Toulouse. From there, many prisoners were transported to concentration camps in Poland, including Auschwitz and Buchenwald.

Alice knew the situation was becoming dire for Jewish families.

"Please, mademoiselle," Elsa grabbed her hand in desperation. "Please, save my children. I heard you find hiding places for Jewish children. The raids have already begun and I'm afraid the Nazis will find us. My husband was taken into the French Civilian Corps when we lived in Paris. We have not heard from him in more than a year."

"Madame Sperber," Alice looked into her hopeless eyes. "The Nazis are everywhere and the French Police are colluding with them. Where am I going to hide these two children when the orphanages are full?"

## Live and Be Counted

"Please, mademoiselle," Elsa pleaded. "I cannot return to the apartment with my children. The smallest indiscretion will give them away. The Nazis will surely find them. Please, help me."

Alice Resch put her hand on top of Elsa's and without much explanation said, "Give me the girl, while you and your son wait here. I'm going to bring her to the Petites Soeurs des Pauvres orphanage to the south of the city. The order of nuns who run Soeurs des Pauvres have already taken in a few children. I will get them to bring in your little girl as well."

"You'll take her to an orphanage?" Elsa repeated with a hopeful relief wrapped in apprehension.

"Yes, that's where I'll take her, as long as the orphanage has room and can take her in. As Alice came from around her desk and reached her arms out to take Helgi, Elsa hesitated at the alarming horror of releasing her daughter to a woman she met only minutes before. However, Elsa felt she was running out of options and could not risk have them discovered by the Nazis. Elsa suddenly came face to face with the unthinkable dilemma of trusting her daughter's life to a strange woman that would bring her to an orphanage she knew nothing about, knowing dreadfully of the prospect of never seeing her again.

Elsa turned away from Alice's reach and tightened her arms around Helgi, reconsidering the absurd idea of having her whisked to an orphanage.

Alice pleaded, "You must give her to me if we're going to hide her. Madame Sperber, you can trust me." Alice came closer to Elsa and wrapped her arms around the mother and daughter, physically transmitting a palpable sense of benevolence and trust. In a surreal loss of control, Elsa surrendered the strong clutch of her arms and let Helgi go into the cradle of Alice's shoulder.

## Chapter 19

"Please God! Please forgive me!" Elsa cried as tears flowed uncontrollably from her eyes. "Please protect my little girl. Please God, bring her back to me. Please protect her!"

Helgi also felt the separation from her mother's grip into the arms of a stranger and, even at a young aged, detected a defining loss was unrolling. "Mama!" Helgi screamed. "Mama! "Mama!"

Three years of memories reeled through Elsa's head. Helgi's birth in Vienna and crawling on the shop floor. The train ride to Paris and strolling her to synagogue. Bullets whizzing through the air on the way Bordeaux and awaiting her visits each day in the hospital after surgery. The footage played over and over in those brief moments, her sweet voice calling her name, becoming louder and sharper with each cry.

"Mama! Come back!" Helgi cried. "Mama! Don't go!"

Elsa let her tears fall uncontrollably as her little daughter was pulled away further and further from her. She was paralyzed, unable to move or think, but deep down she was out of options and could not risk the Nazis discovering them in Toulouse. Yet, it was all happening so quickly. Elsa ran toward the doorway and jumped in front of Alice.

"Please, let me just say goodbye, one more time." Elsa comforted Helgi one last time with kisses and lullaby, not knowing herself whether she would ever see her daughter again.

"Mama!" Helgi continued to cry. "Stay with me, Mama! Don't leave me!"

"My sweet girl," Elsa leaned to kiss Helgi's forehead. "I'm so sorry. Please forgive me. Alice will bring you someplace safe. I promise, we will see each other soon."

## Live and Be Counted

Alfons' body shook as well, witnessing the ghastly act of a mother releasing her baby into the arms of a stranger. He felt his own eyes well and tried to hold back the stream of tears that inevitably followed. He and Helgi had written their own chapters of shared experiences together, fortified by the two months when he cared for her on his own while his mother recovered in the hospital.

The cries continued as Alice brought Helgi from the office and into the car. She felt that the longer they prolonged the goodbye, the more difficult it would be for everyone.

"I'm bringing her to the orphanage, wait here. I'll be back as soon as I can."

Alfons and Elsa watched Alice drive off, holding each other tightly in a sea of sobs and anxiously waiting for Alice to come back. Elsa repeatedly questioned herself and the moral liability she would carry for giving up her daughter, but Alfons sat by her side with unending reassurance that it was the right decision to hide her in the orphanage.

So much so, he began believing it himself.

When Alice arrived back at the office nearly two hours later, Alfons knew it was his turn to part from his mother and say goodbye. Alfons and his mother embraced and the tears began to gush again. She tried to reassure Alfons that this was temporary until the war ended and they could be reunited together with his father.

"There is a boys' orphanage in Levignac twenty-five kilometers from here, I'm going to take your son there," Alice said convincingly as she held her doubts to herself. The orphanage was for boys up to twelve years of age and Alfons was already fourteen. He was tall with visible signs of red stubble around his face, and

## Chapter 19

would be more likely to pass as a young man at the end of his teenage years than at the beginning.

Sister Louise of Les Souers de St. Vincent de Paul orphanage greeted Alice pleasantly as she pulled into the circular driveway beyond the gates. Her expression turned more hostile, however, when she saw a boy sitting in the back seat and knew Alice's true intentions for coming. Sister Louise motioned for Alfons to stay in the car as she took Alice around to the courtyard of the orphanage where the children were playing before dinner time.

"Look at my small boys," Sister Louise said to Alice. "He would be like a cuckoo in a sparrow's nest! I wish I could take him to repay the Quakers for all their help, but it just won't work."

"Are you sure?" Alice pleaded. "Are you sure you can't take him in? He has nowhere to go. He'll end up in a labor camp, or possibly dead, if we cannot hide him here."

"Wait here for me, I'll be right back," Sister Louise told Alice as she disappeared into the chapel. Alice was beginning to shiver in her summer dress amidst the cooling temperatures of the late afternoon.

Sister Louise returned to the courtyard with the Father Secretary and they walked together back to the car where Alfons was still seated. "Please, young man," the Father Secretary instructed Alfons. "Step out from the car."

Alfons did as he was told. As he stepped out, he looked as if he wanted to apologize for being alive. The Father Secretary looked him up and down, stroked his chin and nodded. He turned to Alice and said, "I want you to bring this boy to the monastery La Trappe de Saint Marie in Bellegarde about thirty kilometers north of Toulouse. Ask to speak to the Abbot and tell him that I sent you.

## Live and Be Counted

The boy looks too old to be in our orphanage and surely he will stand out to the police if they raid our premises."

Alfons tried hard to understand the Father Secretary, but did not hear and comprehend everything that was being spoken. When the conversation appeared to end, Alice signaled for Alfons to return to the car and began driving back to the main road wrapped with grass meadows and farmhouses.

After a forty-minute journey on narrow dirt roadways that were wrapped with meadows and occasional farmhouses, they arrived at a large complex of buildings that resembled a small castle at the crest of a hill. The complex was surrounded by large trees and wide-open fields. Alice navigated the car through the gated entrance where she was escorted inside to the parlor by several men in long, brown tunics. Alfons once again remained in the car.

The parlor monk of the monastery greeted Alice and acknowledged the humanitarian work being performed by the Quakers, despite the difficult conditions. Alice explained the plight of the boy in the car and her reason for bringing him to the monastery.

"You can't possibly expect us to hide him!" he exclaimed back to her. "He's only fourteen years old and there are only fully grown men here. Why would the orphanage send you to us?" he asked rhetorically.

Alice brought the parlor monk to the car and pointed to Alfons still sitting in the back seat. "Does he look like a young child to you?"

The parlor monk turned back to Alice. "Wait here momentarily."

## Chapter 19

Waiting alongside her car, Alice was fretful. She did not have a next move, except to bring Alfons back to his mother in Toulouse, which almost certainly would have resulted in his finding and their arrest.

The parlor monk returned with a tall, handsome man in his mid-thirties holding a folded brown tunic in his arms. The man, himself wearing a dark robe, peered inside the car and motioned for Alfons to step out, impressed by the size and maturity in his face as he emerged. "This young man is a fourteen-year-old who can pass as twenty," the Abbot said to the parlor monk, and turning to Alfons, handed him the brown tunic. Alice watched approvingly as the Abbott wrapped Alfons in the tunic and helped him tie a beige rope around his waist. "There's another Jewish man in our care, hiding as a monk-in-training, but secrecy is paramount and you will not know of each other."

Alfons shook his hands from out of the tunic's sleeves and looked up at the large, blue-toned stones of the fortress-like monastery. He turned to Alice and thanked her, but it was nothing more an empty platitude. Deep inside, he could not have felt any more alone, having been swiftly dropped in a remote, forested areas in southern France, thrown into an estranged world where he would take on an identity of a persona he knew nothing about.

A lump of fear formed mightily in his throat as he reluctantly tied the belt around the tunic, as if tying the knot of the belt was a symbol of permanency for his new predicament. Misgivings and doubts plagued his mind, but there was no ability to turn back. Alice was already in her car backing up from the driveway and leaving the compound.

As Alice drove away, the horrific realization occurred to Alfons that the four members of the Sperber family, the people who would always matter most to him, were each separated from one another, far, far away from their home in Vienna. He wanted to cry out in fear and lonesomeness. He wanted to allow the growing wails from within to wash away the burgeoning pain that was growing by the moment. He came across as a young adult to others, but he was still a fourteen-year-old boy ripped from his family in a childhood that was shattered by the Nazis.

Alfons knew not to show vulnerability and forced himself to swallow the visceral cries accumulating inside. As much pain and lonesomeness that he felt walking into the cold vastness of the monastery, he could not imagine the heartache that his mother was feeling having returned to an empty apartment without her two children and without her husband, not knowing if she or any of the people she loved would be uncovered by the Nazis and confronted with death.

## Chapter 20

May 31, 2020

"Hi Papa," Eli positioned his iPad on the kitchen table to the left of the omelet and toast he made for himself that Sunday morning, ten days since their last discussion. "How was your *Shabbat*?" he asked.

"Thanks, Eli. It was fine, but very quiet here for me and Grandma Phyllis," Papa answered. "We're still not allowed to attend synagogue. We took a couple of walks, once in the morning and once in the afternoon. We sat at a bench in one of the parks where we saw children playing on the swings. Everyone was wearing masks."

"Same by us and people are starting to get creative with their masks. At first, we wore the disposable hospital masks. Now people are wearing different colored washable masks, some with the logo of their school or favorite sports team."

"There is definitely a market for everything, isn't there?" Papa asked rhetorically.

"Papa, can I ask you something?" Eli gingerly began to set up a question that he instinctively knew might be a difficult topic to talk about.

"Sure Eli, what is it?"

"Before going to bed last night, my parents were watching the news of people marching in the streets. My father told me that a Black man died from suffocation a few days ago after a police officer kept him on the ground with his knee to his neck."

### Live and Be Counted

"I've been watching the news too," Papa said. "It saddens me that such a thing could happen in America, especially in the year 2020. It brought back the horrors of the Gestapo's brutality in Vienna, beating up and in many cases killing Jews for the smallest or sometimes even no infraction."

"Papa, why are so many people protesting in the streets when they are supposed to be social distancing?" Eli was struggling with the contradictions unfolding on TV.

Papa hesitated as he considered his response. "Unfortunately, this isn't the first instance of a Black man dying under police custody. When the people who are supposed to protect us cause harm, it ripples through many parts of society. If I could, I'd be marching against social injustice too."

"These protests are all large gatherings, aren't people worried about catching COVID-19?" Eli asked.

"I suppose that people are feeling frustrated and hopeless, with many having lost their jobs from government orders to shut down," Papa said. "In some cases, minority groups have been hit harder by the economic effects of the pandemic, which is also revealing a widening gap of economic inequality over the last few months."

"Papa, what do you mean by that? What is economic inequality?"

"Economic inequality refers to the idea people are not all given the same opportunities. Blacks were only granted the same civil rights and legal protections as whites in 1964, around fifteen years after I came to this country," Papa said. "To think that I had these rights when I arrived in New York in 1948, but Black people, who have been living in America for over three-hundred years, did not."

## Chapter 20

Eli knew what civil rights were, he had learned about them in his social studies class this past year. He knew that they were the foundation of America and protected individuals' freedoms."

"Before 1964," Papa added, "Black people could be refused service at a restaurant, denied a job or prevented from attending school simply because of their skin color. They did not even have the right to vote. The Civil Rights Act of 1964 aimed to eradicate discrimination from our society, not just for Blacks, but for all people who differ based on their race, gender, age or religion. As Jews, we sometimes take for granted the religious freedoms we have in America. Blacks today still feel the effects of discrimination, even more than fifty-five years after the passage of the Civil Rights Act."

"Jews have also been discriminated against," Eli waged his own protest. "Look what happened in Europe. Six million Jews were killed by the Nazis, which were voted into power by the German people!"

Since coming to America, Alfons was grateful that Jews were treated fairly and without fear of repression by the government. He also feared that, even in one of the strongest democracies in the world, elected leaders could be voted into power by a majority of people who could repeal laws that were intended to fight discrimination. He lived with constant worry that that America could one day become an inhospitable place for Jews, like it was for them in Europe.

"Do you think our President today is good for the Jews?" Eli asked bluntly.

"The President," Papa offered, "is good for the Jews, if being good to the Jews is ultimately good for the President. That means that if he no longer receives the political credit for his actions, he may not go out of his way to support Jewish interests, here in the United States or through his support of Israel."

"In the last few years, the President has declared Jerusalem as Israel's capital by moving the US embassy and he's helping to broker peace treaties with countries that previously have not recognized Israel's independence. However, even all these actions combined have not increased American Jewish support for the current President," Papa replied.

"Why would Jews not support the President after all that he's done to support Jewish interests in America?" Eli asked confused.

Papa lifted his hand and stroked his chin for a few moments in introspection. "Jews know from their shared, historic experiences that governments can turn quickly against them and trigger anti-Semitic tsunamis. Jews in the United States today are afraid of a President who does not unambiguously condemn race supremacy and violence against minority groups. After all, Jews in America are very much a minority group."

Papa explained to Eli that leading up to the passage of the Civil Rights Act, many Jewish activists marched alongside Martin Luther King Jr. and fought fervently in favor of social equality for Black Americans.

"Jews know all too well what it's like to be discriminated against and have demonstrated their support through political activism and financial lobbying to other groups deserving of social justice and equality. As American Jews, we are most safe when all minority groups feel safe and are afforded the same opportunities. If some groups are emboldened to feel superior over others, racial divide becomes more severe."

"Isn't that what led to Hitler's rise in Germany?" Eli asked.

## Chapter 20

"Yes, to a great extent," Papa answered. "Groups like Jews that were deemed inferior by the majority were ultimately persecuted, driven-out or killed. That's why it's so important for the President to denounce racial and social injustices. We should be weary of leaders who don't do enough to protect the rights of minority groups and vote for leaders who are committed to social equality, since that is ultimately what is in our best interest, too."

"Papa, I think I know who you will vote for," Eli resolved.

"I think you're right!" Papa mused. "I just hope I'll be able to cast my vote in November when Election Day is here."

# Chapter 21

April 1941

"*Eich korim l'cha?*"

Alfons was sitting on the side of the bed, his feet resting barefoot on the cold, unfinished concrete floor beneath him while he was looking through a book about St. Benedict that the Abbott had given. He had taken Alfons down several flights of wide, stone staircases that were dimly lit, leading to the cellar of the monastery, into a windowless room that was teeming with fleas.

Alfons had already unpacked the few articles of clothing he had brought with him and placed them into the drawer of a brown chest next to a matching desk that stood opposite his bed. He pulled his *t'fillin* out from his backpack and placed them into the middle drawer of the chest. A pull-string lamp wrapped in a web of spider silk sat lifeless on the desk. Alfons' eyes followed the spider webs from the lamp to the top of the wall and traced its creepy expanse across the ceiling. He wondered when the last time the room was used, or even cleaned. He found several towels and sheets in the top drawer that he presumed were his to use. There was a narrow aisle between the bed and furniture that was wide enough for just one person to walk.

When he was first brought to his room, Alfons remembered passing a small janitorial closet at the beginning of the hallway. He found a bottle of Javelle water solution, the strongest cleaning agent in the closet, and used it with one of the towels to scrub the walls and surfaces. The smell was near-

## Chapter 21

noxious, but the fleas would have eaten him alive if he slept just one night in the room with them.

"*Eich korim l'cha?*" the man asked again, in a deeper, more seasoned voice than the first time, this time lifting his nose to the unfamiliar smell of sodium chloride and bleach wafting through the doorway.

When he heard the familiar assembly of Hebrew consonants and vowels, Alfons became startled as if he were hearing voices in his head. Alfons recognized the man in the doorway as the one who motioned him out of the car and fitted him with a brown tunic. "What is my name?" he asked quizzically back, translating the phrase in his head, as he turned to the tall, dark figure shadowing in the doorway.

It had been four years since he sat at a classroom desk in Hebrew language class at Stern Yeshiva in Vienna. Now hiding in a small, dark basement room in a monastery perched at the top of a hill, nestled in the soaring trees in southern France, Alfons least expected to hear someone asking what his name was in Hebrew.

"*Kein, tza'ir. Eich korim l'cha?*" the tall man in a brown robe repeated a third time.

"My name?" he stammered. "My name, my name is Alfons."

The tall man let out of laugh. "Oh, even I know that every Jewish boy is given a Hebrew name when they are born. The name by which you are called up as a *Bar Mitzvah* to the *Torah*. The name that links you back to your heritage. The name by which you cannot hide your Judaism. So tell me young man, *eich korim l'cha?*"

This time, Alfons stood up from his bed and confidently turned to the man in the doorway, "*Shem sheli Reuven.*"

**Live and Be Counted**

"Reuven," the man repeated. "Reuven, the first son of the patriarch Jacob? That is a fine name for a strong boy like you, surely also the first born in your family?"

"Yes, that's right," Alfons answered. "My little sister Helgi is only four and she's being hidden in an orphanage near Toulouse. Alfons still could not comprehend how the monk standing in front of him was conversing in Hebrew. "How do you know to speak Hebrew? Are you Jewish?"

The Abbott laughed again, "No, no. I'm not Jewish. I'm a Catholic Monk and I follow the three religious vows of St. Benedict. First, obedience to Jesus Christ. Second, being an instrument of God's work. Third, stability to commit myself to the monastery for the remainder of my life."

"As a young man, I traveled to Jerusalem to study the rules of St. Benedict, delving deep into its sources and showing my dedication to the monk society around me. After five years of study, I earned the right to become an Abbot and was sent back to France to oversee this monastery. My role is to teach the students who wish to dedicate their lives similarly to St. Benedict as I have. Living in Jerusalem for as long as I did, I learned to read and speak Hebrew."

"Can I ask you what an Abbot is?" Alfons inquired.

"Actually, I was going to ask if you could tell me what an Abbot is!" the man replied.

Alfons thought for a moment. Is it possible he already knew? He never heard the term before, but it sounded familiar. "Does *Abbot* come from the same word as *abba*?" He was referencing the word which meant *father* in Hebrew.

"It most certainly does, Reuven," the Abbot called him by his Biblical namesake. "In fact, *abba* pre-dates modern Hebrew

## Chapter 21

and is rooted in ancient Aramaic, the language in which your Talmud is written."

Alfons understood the reference, and although he had never studied directly from the *Talmud*, its teachings and principles were part of the lessons that permeated throughout his Jewish education in school, in synagogue and at home.

"An Abbot," the middle-aged monk continued, "is an ecclesiastical title given to the head of a monastery, like the rabbi of a synagogue. I am the Abbot of this monastery and my job is to help shepherd the young men living here into fine monks, dedicated to our communal, monastic way of life."

"What does your communal way of life look like?" Alfons had many more questions to ask, but he needed to start somewhere.

"In older monastic communities," the Abbot continued, "monks were divided into two groups called lay brothers and choir monks. The primary work of the choir monks was prayer, while the lay brothers provided the material needs of the community by growing food, preparing meals and maintaining the grounds. In our monastery, there is little distinction and responsibilities are divided amongst all of the monks evenly."

"This distinction arose historically because monks who could read Latin typically became choir monks, while monks who were illiterate or could not read Latin became lay brothers. In our monastery, we recite prayers in the vernacular French so that everyone can participate and contribute to the communal needs. Including you," the Abbot added.

"Can anyone become a Catholic monk?" Alfons asked.

"To become a monk, one must first become a postulant by living at a monastery to evaluate what life as a monk is like. As a postulant, you are not bound by any vows and are free to leave the monastery at any time. If the monastic community agrees that the postulant is worthy of being a monk, he begins to participate more fully in the life of the monastery and is given temporary vows. After a few years, the monk then professes permanent vows which are binding for life. Since we dedicate our lives to God, we also take a vow not to marry."

"So tell me Reuven," the Abbot continued with a more intense focus on Alfons. "What do you know about your namesake?"

Alfons tried to remember as much as he could about Jacob and his sons from his Judaic classes at Stern Yeshiva. He knew Reuven was the first son and seemed to be more notoriously associated with the sale of his younger brother Joseph as a slave to Egyptian merchants. "I don't think Reuven was recalled for anything propitious," he admitted. "Or was he?" he asked the Abbot.

"When Jacob was nearing death and it came time to bestow blessings on his children, he seems to give Reuven more of a harsh rebuke than a promising benediction," the Abbot said. He opened the book that he was holding and thumbed through the first one hundred or so pages. The Abbot scrolled the text from the top of the page with his finger and proceeded to recite the biblical verse halfway down.

*"Reuven, you are my firstborn and my strength, but you are hasty like the rush of water."*

Alfons repeated the passage in his head, silently motioning the words with his lips.

"Do you know what this blessing means?" the Abbot turned to Alfons.

## Chapter 21

Alfons shook his head and suddenly felt woefully unprepared understanding his own biblical namesake. He wondered to himself how the Abbot was able to find the passage with such ease.

"Reuven should have been entitled to the kingship and become the undisputed leader of the Israelites," the Abbot stated. "Throughout the stories in which Reuven was a focal character, his decision making was impetuous and sometimes clouded. Despite his first-born status, Jacob did not think Reuven was capable of rising to effective leadership over all of his sons."

"Reuven had flaws, just like we all have shortcomings. By Jacob being realistic with Reuven, he wasn't criticizing him for being hasty, but rather blessing his son with clarity and awareness which would help him and future generations overcome their blind spots of patience and judgement."

Alfons was enjoying this insight from the Abbot, "I never heard this explanation before."

The Abbot continued, "To know your faults is a great thing, but woe is the person who is not aware of those things that can become his stumbling block. Bringing awareness to someone's shortcomings is not an easy thing to do. However, when it's done sincerely, candor can be the most important thing we can do to help others achieve their personal goals in this world."

"I appreciate that," Alfons said. "It must have been hard for a father to tell that to his son, but even harder for a son to hear it from a father. Why are you telling all of this to me?"

The Abbot replied, "Reuven, there are dangerous people out there looking to annihilate good, innocent people like you, simply because they believe differently and superiorly. It may be hard to hear the following message, like it was hard for Reuven to hear the message from his father Jacob. I believe God brought you to our monastery since He has bigger plans for you. It's not your destiny to die at the hands of the Nazis."

"I miss my family," Alfons admitted profoundly, "and I don't know if I'll ever see them again."

"We're going to hide you here for as long as we can, you will live amongst the monks, be one of us. You'll learn about the St. Benedict vows and our ways of living. I'll teach you math and history, as best as I can."

"I would like that," Alfons said. "I think this will be my sixth school in three years."

The Abbot put his arm around Alfons. "Tell me, Reuven, what other questions do you have for me?"

Alfons was trying to process everything about the monks that he just heard. It was a lot to take in and he found it difficult to draw similarities with his own religious life, one that encouraged being a part of society around him, not isolating from it as the monks did.

He went with a more basic discussion. "You mentioned that food is grown here in the monastery?" Surely Alfons must have misheard since he lived in large cities his entire life and did not know the first thing about growing food.

"In a monastery," the Abbot explained, "we are self-sufficient and do not rely on any outside sources for sustenance. That means we grow our own wheat, fruit and vegetables. We also maintain a farm with cows that produce milk and hogs that are served as meat to the community. You'll be expected to participate in the daily chores on the farm and in the fields."

At the mention of meat, Alfons knew he would be faced with decisions that intersected with religious practice and survival.

## Chapter 21

He was grateful that the Abbot had agreed to hide him as a monk within the monastery, but did he expect Alfons to become a monk or just pretend to act as one?

"For my entire life I ate only kosher," Alfons said. "Do you know what kosher is?"

"I do," the Abbot responded. "Observant Jews only eat animals that were ritually slaughtered under a rabbi's supervision."

"We also don't eat dairy products with meat," Alfons continued.

The Abbot responded understandably. "From my years in Jerusalem, I know very well about the laws of eating kosher. You may be tempted time to time, but I'm sure we can create a balanced menu of cheeses, vegetables and other proteins that will enable you to honor the dietary traditions of your faith."

Alfons was comforted. As nice as the Abbot was, Alfons needed to be independently strong in his faith. Neither his mother nor father were around to set expectations or to remind him of the rituals, the prayers or the holidays. Alfons reckoned that he was on his own to exercise his religious faith to the best of his ability. If he was going to avoid eating non-kosher meat, he would need to find the strength to demonstrate this commitment early on and without deviation.

The Abbot informed Alfons that he would come back the next evening to begin their studies. As he retreated from the room through the doorway, he turned back to Alfons and sniffed the lingering Javelle fragrance in the room. "You know," the Abbot said, "up until a few minutes ago, the stone walls in this room were never washed in the one hundred years since the monastery was built. Let's hope they don't crumble under the chemical strength of the Javelle you just applied! If they don't, I have thirty more rooms that could use scrubbing!"

The Abbot turned a half-smile at his sarcastic truism, bid his goodnight and walked out of the room, leaving Alfons insufferably alone with his thoughts and fears once again.

## Chapter 22

June 15, 2020

"Eli, the Internet is an amazing invention." Alfons knew that with the arrival of warm weather and the government loosening some of the lockdown restrictions on outdoor activities, he would be competing more for Eli's attention on Zoom. They were still having their virtual chats, but not as frequently as they did in April and May when lockdown orders were unswerving.

Eli wasn't about to disagree with Papa's proclamation about the Internet, but it seemed rather random after all this time Zooming together. The life that he knew always had the Internet. "Papa, saying the Internet is amazing is like saying how great cars, washing machines and cell phones are. They exist and everyone has them, but no one says how wonderful those inventions are were anymore."

For most of Alfons' adult working life, he sold the newest refrigerators, dishwashers, televisions, stereo systems and video recorders. He needed to have a pulse on the latest technologies if he was going to be a successful appliance salesman. The store extended him a discount to purchase floor models so he could become more familiar their features. As a secondary benefit, he drew admiration from his neighbors, his children and their friends whenever he came home with something new that hadn't yet become a common household item.

"The Internet is different," Papa declared. "It can bring the farthest reaches of the Earth into your house and it can connect us in ways we could never be connected before."

## Live and Be Counted

"Papa, just think about how the Internet has kept all of us connected during the pandemic!" Eli marveled. "We can even go to school from our bedrooms!"

During the pandemic, everyone was increasing their reliance on the Internet for entertainment, work, shopping and school. It was frightening to realize that people no longer needed to leave their homes to maintain functional and productive lives. Eli wondered if that would become the new normal even after the pandemic ended.

"For years, I did not know anything about the woman who brought me to the monastery. I never saw her again, never had an opportunity to thank her. In 1998, when I reached my seventies, I had the cable company install Internet wires in my house. That year was also the fiftieth anniversary of my immigration to the United States and I became curious to research more about my years in Europe. I did not remember the name or location of the monastery, but I did remember a morsel about the woman who my mother begged to save me. Her name was Alice and she worked for a Quaker organization, helping displaced children during the war."

"The Quaker organization? As in the company that makes oatmeal and granola bars?" Eli asked calling forward a mental image of an older man with white hair and a blue hat who adorned an array of breakfasts and snacks in his pantry.

Papa laughed. "In 1681, King Charles II of England gave William Penn a large land grant in America as a religious sanctuary for Quakers who were being persecuted in Europe."

"So is Quaker a type of religion?" Eli was still confused what the group represented and trying to decipher the connection to the food company.

## Chapter 22

"Quakers are a branch of Christianity," Papa explained. "Many Quakers fled Europe in the 1600s and 1700s to settle in what became Philadelphia where William Penn helped create a safe place for them to live without fear."

"Sounds like the state of Pennsylvania was named after William Penn," Eli remarked.

"It sure was," Papa responded. "I discovered the Quaker headquarters in Philadelphia using the Internet and decided to contact them through an email address that was listed on their website. I asked them if they knew someone by the name of Alice who had hidden Jewish children during the war."

"Did someone respond to your email?" Eli asked, thinking it was a long shot anyone in Philadelphia would know a woman named Alice from Europe without much else to describe her. He reasoned that if Papa was around seventy in 1998, Alice must have been in her eighties or nineties, if she was even alive.

"I received a call after a few days from a man named Jack Sutters who promised to look into it and get back to me. About a week later he did!" Eli sensed the elation in Papa's voice. "When he called back, he told me that a woman named Alice Resch Synnestvedt lived in Denmark and had been honored by *Yad Vashem*, which is the National Holocaust Museum in Israel, for her life-risking work to save Jewish children in southern France during the war."

"Was it the same person?" Eli asked with anticipation.

"I knew it had to be!" Papa said excitingly. "Mr. Sutters told me that she was still alive and gave me her mailing address. We both guessed that she probably did not use email. Anyway, I wrote her a letter and told her that I had been living near Toulouse with my mother and asked if she was the woman who hid my sister in an orphanage and hid me in the monastery."

### Live and Be Counted

"Did you hear back from Alice after you wrote to her?"

"I did and Alice told me that she remembered me too!" Papa exclaimed, no longer holding back his exhilaration. She remembered taking me to an orphanage for boys that turned me away because I looked too old, and she also recalled pleading with the Abbot to hide me in the monastery. She did not know what had happened to us afterwards and was thrilled to learn that we had survived the war. She included her phone number in the letter and I called her several times in Denmark to talk."

"That's an amazing story, I can't believe you found the woman who saved you," Eli voiced.

"Wait, there is more!" Papa was bursting with excitement. "Alice gave me the number of another man that she was also responsible for saving. Hal Myers was living in Myrtle Beach, South Carolina. I contacted him and learned that there were more than a dozen other Holocaust survivors living in the US who traced their survival to the heroic actions of Alice Resch Synnestvedt."

"Were they all hidden in the monastery like you were," Eli asked.

"I always suspected there was another Jewish man hiding in the monastery and disguised as a monk, but I never knew for sure. During the early years of World War Two, Alice took part in humanitarian missions to deliver aid to child refugees in the labor camps in France. During these efforts, she was able to obtain visas for several children who became orphaned and could be fostered by relatives living in the United States. When word surfaced that the Nazis were beginning to transport Jewish prisoners to concentrations camps, Alice was able to smuggle about fifty children into orphanages, hiding them on various occasions in the trunk of her car."

"Did those children survive the war?" Eli asked.

## Chapter 22

"I don't know about everyone, but for all of us who did we owe our lives to the courageous actions of Alice Resch," Papa proudly said. "After I contacted Hal Myers in Myrtle Beach, we decided to invite Alice to a reunion with her survivors. Many had already discovered her in earlier years and had taken trips to Denmark to reunite in person. In 2002, when Alice was ninety-four, the reunion came together and she flew to North Carolina with a personal health aide to meet a dozen or so men and women that she was responsible for hiding during the war."

"Truly amazing," Eli listened in awe.

"A year after the reunion in Myrtle Beach, Grandma Phyllis and I took a trip to visit Alice in Denmark. She passed away a few years later, but I'm forever grateful for having discovered her. As part of the second leg of our trip to Denmark, we traveled to Israel and found the tree that was planted in her honor outside the children's memorial at *Yad Vashem*."

"The *Talmud* says that someone who saves a single life is as if they have saved the entire world. Alice did just that."

"Papa," Eli asked, "did you ever find the Abbot from the monastery?"

In 1997, Alfons and Phyllis indeed traveled to France to retrace his steps in and around Toulouse. They located the orphanage where Helgi had been hidden since that was near the city. A lady at the tourist center in Toulouse mapped out eleven or twelve abbeys, convents, monasteries, and nunneries within fifty kilometers of Toulouse. They drove to each one using an old-fashioned folding paper map and eventually followed a narrow winding road to the top of a secluded hill.

"It looked abandoned, but I knew it was the monastery where I was hidden. We walked around, knocked on the doors and peeked through the windows. There didn't seem to be anyone there anymore," Papa said.

"When we returned home, I Googled the monastery but nothing relevant came up. The only thing that I found was a postcard picture of the monastery from 1908. The monastery must have closed at some point after the war. I never knew what happened to the Abbot."

# Chapter 23

June 1942

Living in the monastery, Alfons blended in with the other monks. He awoke early each morning and minded his duties in the field, planting seeds during the spring season, running irrigation lines in the summer and picking fruits, wheat stalks and vegetables in the autumn. He spent afternoons on the dairy farm milking cows and harvesting chicken eggs.

During breaks, Alfons would usually help cook meals in the kitchen. Occasionally, he stayed in the fields reading a book while the other monks went to prayer. His complexion and ginger hair maintained a strong, vibrant color from the time he spent outdoors in the sun, despite the time spent in his windowless bedroom.

Keeping up with progress of the war, however, proved difficult since there were limited connections to the outside world. Alfons did not know anyone who owned a radio and never saw any newspapers at the monastery. He sometimes asked the Abbot if he had heard anything about the war, but only received short soundbites, none of which could really be verified.

Alfons heard that London was being bombed by German planes flying across the English Channel. Italy had joined the war as a German ally and the United States was becoming involved after being bombed by Japan. Alfons wasn't sure why Japan was involved in the war altogether.

Alfons did not know what was happening to the Jewish communities in Vienna or Paris, how his mother and sister were faring or the fate of his father. The anxiety of not knowing how long he would need to remain alone and hidden in the monastery made for long, sleepless and fitful nights.

Alfons fulfilled the commitments he made to himself when he was first brought to the monastery by wearing his *t'fillin* and not eating meat or chicken that he knew was not kosher. He tried to observe the *Shabbat* day of rest each week, but this was more difficult since he did not feel comfortable evading the fieldwork or cooking duties, which also may have outed his identify as a Jewish boy.

Marking the Jewish holidays and its rituals proved even more difficult as he lost track of the calendar that designated when they fell during the year. He knew Passover was usually celebrated in April and that the start of the holiday coincided with the beginning of the Jewish month of Nissan, which followed the lunar cycle. He observed the waxing of the moon each night until it was full, signaling the start of Passover. For eight days, he declined to eat bread, which was forbidden during the holiday to commemorate the Israelites who left Egyptian slavery in haste without time for their dough to rise. In September when the moon was undetectable, he figured it to be the start of Rosh Hashanah, the Jewish New Year and the ten-days of repentance that culminated with a fast on Yom Kippur, the holiest day of the year.

"Alfons, you do know that we have prayer mass between seven and eight o'clock each night after dinner," the Abbot would say more than once toward the end of their study sessions. "I would love to see you there one time. It's a beautiful service and many of the brothers you work with in the fields have melodious voices that lead us in choir mass."

"Thank you, Father." Alfons responded. "I will try my best to come." The Abbot had been so nice to him for all this time and Alfons felt he could no longer show disrespect to the Abbot by continuing to decline his personal invitation.

## Chapter 23

One night, Alfons decided to attend mass, but timed his arrival toward the end of the service. He carried a conflicting feeling of the heart every step of the way and speculated whether his presence would encourage the Abbot and the brothers to convert him away from Judaism to Christianity.

Alfons humbly entered the church that was positioned on the north end of the monastery and found a seat in an empty pew toward the back of the sanctuary. His eyes surveyed the vast room, from the towering walls and pillars on both sides, until they locked in on the Abbot who was leading a prayer from a podium on the front stage. Behind him, stain glass windows made up a large portion of the facade that Alfons surmised were pictures of disciples from Jesus.

Directly behind the Abbot was a sculpture built into the marble fascia showing Jesus Christ on the cross. Alfons had never been inside a church before and he found the stalwart sculpture both beautiful and frightening at the same time. Beautiful in the etchings that meticulously revealed Christ' emotions and frightening in the flood of horrors over some versions of history that have fueled anti-Semitism by claiming Jews, not Romans, were responsible for Christ's death.

Alfons lifted his right hand, gently used it to cover his eyes and recited *Shema Yisrael* through the faint movement of his lips, a ritual he had done with his parents each night since he was three years old before going to bed. The Abbot and the brothers had been kind to him, a young Jewish boy chased from his home and ripped from his family. God had sent him here for protection and he was strengthened being inside of the church knowing those around him were praying to the same God that he was.

After dinner and mass, the Abbot came to Alfons' room as he did almost every evening and thanked him for attending prayers earlier that night.

## Live and Be Counted

"Father, why do you think this is happening to us?" Alfons asked. "What have the Jewish people done to be forced from our homes, hunted by the Germans? You have been so kind to protect me here in the monastery, but there are thousands of us fleeing for our lives."

"Reuven, that is a very difficult question and I wish I knew how to answer you," the Abbot said. "Perhaps we need to look back at the *Torah* for guidance."

Alfons responded with a look of curiosity and, at the Abbot's nod, reached for the Bible that they had been studying together. The Abbot thumbed through most of the pages until he reached a section toward the end.

"God has blessed the Jews in many ways," the Abbot opened, "but, God also predicated certain calamities would fall upon the Jewish people. These are known as the curses in Deuteronomy."

Alfons wasn't aware that the *Torah* contained curses. He shuddered to think what the Abbot was going to show him.

"This section contains one of the most terrifying passages in the Hebrew Bible. In his final days, before the ancient Israelites entered the land of Israel, Moses warned that the people would be dealt a terrible fate if they neglected their covenant with God."

The Abbot scrolled his finger across the page and read the verses in front of him. *"A nation unknown to you will devour the fruit of your ground and all your labor. You will bear sons and daughters, but they will go into captivity. Your life will be filled with dread both night and day, and you will be left few in number."*

Alfons was stunned at the realization that God's rebuke in the Hebrew Bible seemed to be unfolding in front of him. "Do you

## Chapter 23

think Moses was predicting our time, right now? Have we neglected our faith in God?" he asked the Abbot.

"Reuven, reading these verses in the dark backdrop of 1942 can certainly sound like the recital of the terrible fate predicted by the *Torah*. These verses raise very difficult questions. Is God full of anger and retribution? Does God turn the other way at the sufferings of innocents? Could God be preventing the tragedies befalling your people?"

"Undoubtedly, these are difficult questions," the Abbot continued. "No other nation on Earth has grappled with such difficult questions, and yet the Jewish people have done so with courage and resiliency, time and time again. Jewish philosophers from the Medieval Times through the Enlightenment have struggled to answer these questions. For some, it instigated a reason to leave Jewish faith and traditions. For others, it strengthened their resolve and belief."

"How can such questions strengthen someone's faith?" Alfons asked, subconsciously realizing that he himself had enriched his own belief in God against unconscionable conditions.

"Jewish tradition teaches that God answered every question Moses ever asked Him except for the following: *Why do bad things happen to good people?* There is profound comfort knowing that there are some things that will always lie beyond the realm of human understanding. When God doesn't answer our prayers, it doesn't necessarily mean that He doesn't exist. Rather, He may have chosen to say no or to answer them at a later time."

"Could it be that God is choosing to say no to us?" Alfons asked painfully.

"Throughout history, Jewish people have suffered great catastrophes," the Abbot resumed. "The destruction of the Temple and exile from Israel in 70 AD, the Hadrian persecutions in the second century, the murder of Jews in the Crusades during the twelfth and thirteenth centuries, the Spanish Inquisition in the fifteenth century, the blood libels in the sixteenth century, the pogroms in the nineteenth century, and most recently, Kristallnacht."

"All of these events have been inscribed into collective Jewish memory. In each generation, Jewish people have tried to find meaning in the tragedies that befell them. Instead, they were resigned to find moral comparisons with the stories of their biblical patriarchs who experienced anguish during their own lives, such as the sacrificial binding of Isaac by his father, the selling of Joseph to slavery by his brothers, the suffering of Job through the death of his children and loss of his livelihood."

"We learned about those stories together, Father," Alfons reflected on the lessons from each of the stories, none as powerful as the totality in which the Abbot was threading a tapestry of heavenly reward and punishment.

"Perhaps we should be asking a different question entirely?" the Abbot posed daringly. "Rather than asking *Where is God* in His quest for justice, perhaps we should be asking *Where is Man* and his display of gross injustice?"

"Father, where do I go from here?" Alfons was pleading for answers and more guidance. "I have committed myself to practice the *Torah*'s commandments, to honor our rituals, to respect our traditions. Not once did I violate the laws of eating kosher. Not once did I knowingly desecrate the *Shabbat*."

"Reuven, you have been faithful to your beliefs beyond any of the monks I have ever guided," the Abbott agreed. "Just as God predicted calamities for the Jewish people, He also foretold of blessings and promises that I believe will come equally true."

## Chapter 23

For the first time in nearly four years, Alfons looked up with a spark of hope in his eyes. "What type of promises, Father?"

The Abbot turned a couple of pages forward and once again scrolled his finger until he reached another set of verses. *"When you and your children return to the Lord with all your heart, then the Lord will restore your fortunes and have compassion on you. Even if you have been banished to the most distant land under the heavens, from there the Lord your God will gather you and bring you back."*

"I don't understand," Alfons reacted. "How can God fulfill this type of promise when I'm hidden in a dark, windowless room in the basement of a monastery?"

The Abbot allowed a small smile to crease his face. "I cannot say for sure, but I began to witness something miraculous while I was studying in Jerusalem in the late 1920s and early 1930s. Waves of Jews fleeing anti-Semitism were immigrating to Israel. They were coming from Russia. They were coming from Yemen. They were coming from Germany, Poland and Czechoslovakia."

"Alfons, what do you think drew these refugees to a barren, deserted land with no natural resources and no infrastructure?" the Abbot asked rhetorically. "By some estimates, there are more than half a million Jews currently residing in the biblical land of Israel, more than any amount in nearly two thousand years since the exile of the Jews by the Roman Empire in the year 70 AD."

Alfons suddenly remembered learning about Zionism at the Stern Yeshiva, a movement started Theodor Herzl who himself lived in Vienna in the late 1880s, promoting the idea of a Jewish homeland as the only antidote to anti-Semitism for the Jews across Europe.

**Live and Be Counted**

"Theodore Herzl died in his forties, but his political appeals for a Jewish state grew in popularity after his death. During The Great War, the British Empire defeated the Ottomans and took control of a piece of land spanning the eastern bank of the Mediterranean Sea into the Arabian desert, with the Jordan River slicing through the middle. At the start of The Great War, there were less than one hundred thousand Jews living in Israel's ancient cities, most of them indigenous from the Temple Period."

"Following Britain's defeat of the Ottomans, British Foreign Secretary Arthur Balfour issued a Declaration on behalf of the government in 1917 announcing support for the establishment of a national home for the Jewish people, the very first public expression of a Jewish state by a major political power."

"Father, what does all this mean? How does it relate back to God's curses?" Alfons asked.

"Consider the possibility that as God has forewarned the Jewish people about a terrible fate, He is also telling us about a rebirth. I know it's hard to imagine, but perhaps the suffering you're experiencing now is God's way of fulfilling His promise to return Jewish people to its ancient homeland."

"Father," Alfons replied, "it's hard to find any good in the world right now."

"I taught you about Jacob's hidden blessing to his firstborn son. You know, Jacob wasn't the only person to bless Reuven."

Alfons continued to listen intently.

"Moses, at the waning moments of his life, worried that Jacob's removal of Reuven from the firstborn leadership would risk his grandchildren being absorbed into anonymity. The tribe of Reuven did not want to enter the land promised to the Israelites following their sojourn of forty years in the desert. They preferred

## Chapter 23

the pastures on the eastern side of the Jordan River. Moses final words to them was a simple but powerful blessing: *May the tribe of Reuven live and may his people be counted in the number.*"

"I don't understand how that is a blessing," Alfons admitted to the Abbot. "There is little in that blessing about being prosperous or healthy, just that Reuven's tribe be included in a census."

"The message is indeed subtle," the Abbot continued. "What does it mean to live and be counted? You see, each person has opportunities to contribute to society in innumerable ways, sometimes in large quantities and sometimes in small doses. Even though the tribe of Reuven would settle on the eastern side of the Jordan River and not enter the land of Israel, Moses did not want them to become lost from their heritage and forgotten by the other tribes."

"Reuven, my son," the Abbot placed his hand atop Alfons' shoulders. "We don't know what will happen in this war. We don't know where you may find yourself or what God may call upon you to do. Therefore, I wish to convey the same blessing that Moses bestowed upon the tribe of Reuven. No matter where you are, find ways to contribute to your environment. Make a difference in someone else's life. Make sure that you live life to its fullest and that you count to someone else. *Live and be counted*, Reuven. *Live and be counted.*"

A sudden knock at the door broke the intensity of the conversation. The Abbot stood up and opened the door to one of the brothers dressed in a brown robe. Alfons looked up with curiosity. Other than the Abbot, he never had any visitors to his bedroom quarters in the basement. "May we help you?" the Abbot asked the monk, with a shade of irritation from being interrupted.

## Live and Be Counted

"My deepest apologies for disturbing you, Father," the monk begged. "I have been searching almost half an hour to let you know that man arrived in a uniform tonight asking about a Jewish boy hidden in the monastery. I was unable to turn him away and he is waiting adamantly in the refectory."

At the sound of the word *uniform,* Alfons' heart began to race harder than he ever felt it pound before. His breathing became labored and his stomach began to churn. "The Nazis," he whispered to the Abbot. "How? How did they find me?"

"Don't worry, Reuven. We will face this together," the Abbot tried comfort him. "You are a monk amongst the brothers. Put on your robe and tie the belt around your waist." He reached out his hand to Alfons assuredly, but even the Abbot's fear began to swell.

The three of them walked out from the bedroom and paced down the long, dark corridor of the monastery cellar that had become so familiar to Alfons over the past fifteen months. They walked up the wide, dimly lit stone staircase and eventually arrived at the refectory where Alfons had eaten most of his meals. As they approached the entrance, a man sitting at one of the stables pushed back his chair and stood up. He was dressed in a uniform with dark boots, belted pants and a long-sleeve single breasted coat buttoned from the neck to below the naval.

Alfons took a few cautious steps into the refectory and squinted his eyes to make out the shadowy figure. "Father?" he questioned.

The Abbot turned his face to Alfons, reached for his hand and squeezed it in comfort, "I'm here, my son. I'm here."

Surprisingly, the Abbot did not feel Alfons squeeze his hand back and saw that he wasn't looking back at him either. Instead, he was staring ahead at the uniformed man.

"Father!" Alfons cried out again. "Is it really you?"

Alfons dropped the hand of the Abbot and sprinted to the man in the uniform. When he reached him, Alfons draped his arms around his father, tears flowing uncontrollably from his eyes and down his face.

"Yes son, it's me. It's truly me!" Alexander was crying too and he buried his tears into the robe across Alfons' shoulder.

Neither the Abbot nor the brother that accompanied them could overcome their emotions watching the moving reunion between Alfons and his father. They too were locked in arms, wiping the tears from their eyes as they watched the father and son embrace.

"I can't believe you're alive. I thought you were dead. I didn't think I'd ever see you again." Alfons was still sobbing.

Alexander curled a smile through the tears, squeezing his arms around his son. "I've been dreaming of this moment for two years," he said.

"Me too, Father. Me too."

## Chapter 24

June 22, 2020

"Do you think we can come visit you?" Eli asked Papa at the beginning of their next session. "Zoom school is over, we made it through, but unfortunately summer camps have been canceled because of COVID-19."

"I'm sorry, Eli, but it's still not safe. Grandma Phyllis and I are older and our immune systems would be unable to fight coronavirus. We're staying right where we are, no visitors allowed."

"Papa," Eli asked skeptically, "do you ever order take-out food through your phone?"

"Of course we do!" Papa responded. "If I can figure out how to use Zoom, I can place a dinner order online. Just last night, we had kosher Chinese food delivered to us."

"We had Chinese food for dinner last night, too!" Eli roared. "Sweet and sour chicken with the red sauce and white rice is my favorite."

"Mine too!" Papa laughed. "I love a good fortune cookie, but each time I unroll the message, I know that it is really God who is looking out for my fortune. I'll never forget that night seeing my father standing in his uniform in the monastery. I hadn't seen him in almost two years. He was smaller, skinner and older than I remembered, but undoubtedly it was him. I was convinced that he was dead and I'd never see him again, yet there was always a small belief I had in God that he was alive and coming to get me."

## Chapter 24

"How did Grandpa Alexander find you in the monastery? I thought he had been captured by the Nazis?" Eli asked with bated anticipation.

"Leading up to Nazi Germany's invasion of France in May 1940, Father had been drafted into the French military, supplying the soldiers on the frontlines with fresh clothing, food and other provisions. By the middle of June, the French military had lost many soldiers in battle and was at imminent collapse, surrendering to the Germans as they closed in on Paris. An armistice treaty was reached on June 22, 1940 between France and Germany."

"Why did the German's want to create a treaty with France, especially if they had the upper hand?" Eli asked.

"France was a large country and it would have been too difficult for the Germans alone to govern the French on their own territory, especially as the Nazis needed to keep their eyes on England toward the north and west for a possible counter-attack."

Papa continued, "As part of the French surrender, Germany captured two million French soldiers and sent them as prisoners to factories, mines and labor camps where they were enslaved to produce machinery, munitions, food and other provisions needed for the German war effort."

"Was Grandpa Alexander taken as one of those two million prisoners of war?" Eli asked.

"Father was initially interned in the Rivesaltes detention camp in the south of France on the banks of the Balearic Sea. Soon after, he was transferred to the Gurs detention camp in the southwest part of France and was transported back and forth each day to a factory where he worked to produce clothing for the German soldiers."

## Live and Be Counted

"Your father produced clothing for the German soldiers?" Eli repeated. "That's ironic given the scheme he had agreed to with the Gestapo in exchange for his release when you lived in Vienna."

"Father indeed leveraged his skills to keep himself valuable and alive," Papa agreed. "It was his currency to the Nazis. Unfortunately, the conditions in the detention camp were horrible and food was rationed. The sleeping barracks were cold and there were only a few blankets to go around. Of the prisoners that tried to escape, some were successful while many others were shot dead. For two years, Father kept his head down and tried not to draw unnecessary attention from the Nazis. He worked on the clothing lines and tried to stay healthy so he would be of continued use to the Germans."

In the years that followed the Holocaust, firsthand accounts revealed more about the vast network of concentration camps and gas chambers that were being used by the Nazis to execute plans for the Final Solution and mass genocide of European Jewry. Alexander, who was imprisoned in the labor camps in France, was told that he would be transported to an industrial park in Marseille, France where he would sew clothing for the German soldiers.

"Father noticed that the Germans were segregating the Jewish captives from the other French prisoners and feared that their final destination would be concentration camps in Germany or Poland, not Marseille. As they packed their bags, whispers among the Jewish prisoners confirmed their worst fears that they were being sent to Auschwitz."

Eli shivered at the sound of Auschwitz. He knew that Auschwitz was among the most pernicious death camps where Jews were sent to gas chambers thinking they were going to cleanse in showers. If they weren't sent to die in the gas chambers, most met death from starvation, disease or medical experiments.

## Chapter 24

"How did Grandpa Alexander possibly survive Auschwitz?" Eli questioned.

"Father escaped from the Nazis before he ever got to Auschwitz," Papa recounted. "Father wore his grey striped prison garb on the train, but in his bag he packed his French military uniform which he was wearing when he was captured by the Germans and kept hidden in his bunk at Rivesaltes."

Eli tried to imagine himself in the transport, listening to the way Papa described the dark train rumbling along the rails. He tried to picture himself squeezed into a train car with hundreds of prisoners, forced to sit on defecated floors or stand against the wall of the rickety rail car for hours on end.

"The transport train reached Marseille at night where the Jews prisoners were told they would be transferred to another train that was carrying Jews from another labor camp. Father was standing in between two train cars with his suitcase and, as it came to a stop, quickly pulled out the French military uniform pants and slipped it over prisoner scrubs. He finished buttoning his uniform jacket and put the military cap over his head as the train car came to a screeching halt."

Eli's heart was racing.

"As the train door opened, a Nazi officer climbed the few steps into the train. Father saluted him in his native German tongue, *'Guten abend. Heil mein Führer'* and confidently stepped down onto the train platform."

"Grandpa Alexander spoke fluent German and, because it was dark, the Nazis couldn't tell he was one of the French Jews," Eli said astoundingly.

### Live and Be Counted

"Father approached another Nazi officer standing at the beginning of the platform and saluted him as well. *Heil mein Führer*, he said raising an outstretched open palm in allegiance to Hitler. He told the Nazi officer that he spent the last two hours on the train keeping the decorum of the Jewish prisoners and asked him for a cigarette."

"Grandpa Alexander fooled them again!" Eli announced proudly. "Like he did when he slipped through Huber's and Eichmann's hands in Vienna!"

Papa continued, "He put the cigarette in his mouth, thanked the Nazi officer and walked away from the platform."

Alfons continued to describe how his father paced around the perimeter of the station, as if he was on a break, and waited until the transport train to Auschwitz pulled away into the darkness. He shrewdly slipped out of the train station unnoticed and spent the next seven days trekking through farmland and forests along the route of the tracks until he arrived in Toulouse. Alexander survived on wild fruit and nuts, drank water from streams and slept in haystacks of abandoned barns. He journeyed between dusk and dawn, limiting himself to covert movement during the day so that his French uniform would not raise any suspicion.

"Grandpa Alexander went to Toulouse since that's where he told Grandma Elsa to go in 1940, before he was enlisted in the French army," Eli recollected.

"That's right," Papa confirmed. "When he arrived in Toulouse, he was exhausted and famished. He got in contact with Monsieur Victor Martin, his business partner who had picked us up from the train station two years before and brought us to his apartment. The apartment remained in Martin's family name and so the Nazis never suspected that he was hiding Jews. Mother was

## Chapter 24

able to stay in the apartment unscathed and undetected after sending Helgi to the orphanage and me to the monastery."

"Grandma Elsa must have been shocked to see Grandpa Alexander," Eli said.

"Just as I was," Papa said. "After Father met up with Mother, they went to the Quaker offices to seek Alice Resch's help in retrieving me and Helgi."

Alfons explained how Alice had gotten more involved with the French resistance, which in turn was being supported by funding coming from the American Quaker organization in Philadelphia. Alice was personally responsible for saving forty-eight children, hiding them in various orphanages and, in some instances, accompanying them close to the Swiss border, which was accepting a limited number of refugees.

"It was rumored that the German's turned a blind eye to the humanitarian work of the Quakers in southern France since the Quakers had sent funds and relief workers to Germany after World War One."

"You mean The Great War," Eli said, pleased with himself for listening.

"Right, The Great War," Papa smiled. "Alice drove Father to the La Trappe de Saint Marie monastery, which is where we reunited."

As Alfons retold the story of his father's diversion, he was overcome with gratitude to God at the series of miracles, good fortune and wit that enabled him to remain healthy during his internment, escape the train headed to Auschwitz and survive a seven-day journey on foot.

## Live and Be Counted

"So you see, Eli, I never gave up on my faith in God during the time I lived in the monastery. And God never gave up his faith in me."

# Part Four

## Switzerland

## Chapter 25

August 1942

"Alexander, these papers show you are French citizens from Alsace and will help you get to Switzerland," explained Monsieur Martin, whose involvement with the French resistance had accelerated over the last year.

The French Resistance was a collection of movements that fought against the German occupation of France and the collaborationist regime. Resistance cells were small groups of armed men and women who, in addition to their guerrilla warfare activities, were also publishers of underground newspapers, providers of first-hand intelligence information and maintainers of escape networks that helped Jewish victims from Nazi pursuit. The Resistance came from all economic levels and political leanings of French society and played a significant role in facilitating the Allies' rapid advance through France following the invasion of Normandy, providing military intelligence on the German defenses. The Resistance' legacy offered the country with an inspiring example of the patriotic fulfilment of a national imperative countering an existential threat to French nationhood.

"These identification cards afford you the best chance of getting through any checkpoints. The French-Swiss border isn't heavily guarded, but keep these papers on you at all times in case you need to present them to policemen or soldiers you encounter on the way."

Alfons listened intently as Monsieur Martin went through the folio with his father in the apartment living room. They were

## Live and Be Counted

mapping out plans to cross into Switzerland where Jewish refugee camps were being established.

Monsieur Martin continued, "Alsace is a region in northeastern France on the Rhine River bordering Germany. The area has alternated between German and French control over the centuries and reflects a mix of these two cultures, so your Austrian accents as French citizens will go unsuspected if anyone checks your papers."

Alfons was fifteen years old and had lived through experiences that tested his physical and spiritual wellbeing during the last few years. He watched the Nazis humiliate his father and ransack his store. He dodged bullets from German warplanes on the side of the road on the way toward Bordeaux. He took care of his younger sister for two months while his mother recovered from infection in the hospital. He lived as a monk in a windowless room for a year and a half, veiling his identity as a Jew.

Alfons himself had grown wiser, sharpened his decision making and refined his interactions with adults. He had earned a seat in the living room with his father and Monsieur Martin to plan their next steps.

"Will we be safe in Switzerland? Won't the Germans find us there?" Alfons asked.

"Switzerland has maintained its armed neutrality as it did during The Great War twenty-five years earlier," Monsieur Martin explained, conducting a modest history lesson with Alfons to explain why Switzerland was their next hope for sanctuary.

"It's being regarded as a haven for refugees, Jews and Gentiles alike, if you can get there. The neutrality agreement relies on a steady flow of capital and supplies from Switzerland to help Germany finance the war, in exchange that Germany won't occupy Switzerland. The problem is that Switzerland is also under

## Chapter 25

pressure from Germany to curb the number of Jewish refugees entering the country."

"How exactly will we get across the border to Switzerland?" Alfons asked. Their travels from Vienna involved trains, cars, horses, and straightforward walking, and none of the legs of their journeys were without risks.

Monsieur Martin answered, "You are going to buy train tickets at the central station in Toulouse, the same station you arrived at two years ago. The train will bring you to a small town called Evian in the French Alps overlooking Lake Geneva. If you are examined on the train, show them your French identification cards and say you are taking a few days of summer to enjoy Lake Geneva."

"Where will we go when we get across the border?" Alfons asked. Unlike the doubt he raised when his mother implored him to pack his bags when leaving Paris, Alfons knew they could not remain in France so long as the Germans occupied the north and were collaborating with the armistice government in the south. He was exhausted from being on the run for nearly five years since leaving Vienna in 1938.

"There are refugee camps on the Swiss side of the border near a town called Aigle. That's where many are headed, but you'll need get through the Alps and pass into Swiss territory first," Monsieur Martin cautioned as he handed Alexander another envelope.

Alexander peered inside and returned a look with indebted eyes. Before he could say anything, Monsieur Martin broke the silence of gratitude. "Don't thank me," he said. "This is money I owe you from the last several shipments before you were taken into the French Civil Corps. Plus, some additional money on credit for the shipment you will send me when you return." A generous smile curled across his face.

"How could I ever thank you, my friend," Alexander said, extending his arm and consummating with a firm handshake.

"Thank you for lending us your apartment these last two years," Alfons repeated also extending his hand to Monsieur Martin. "I'm not sure what we would have done without your kindness."

Monsieur Martin drove them to the central station in Toulouse and goodbyes were exchanged once again. "When you arrive, you will need to find a guide who will take you through the Alps to the Swiss border. The trails are confusing and dangerous. There is a hefty price, which you will find enough to pay in the envelope I gave you. The guides are crucial for getting through the Alps, most of them are profiteering, but they are a piece of the French resistance."

The four Sperbers, with minimal bags accompanying them, showed their French passports and boarded a train to Evian that took them into the French countryside through Montpellier and Lyon. It was a long train ride, more than fourteen hours and longer than the train that took them from Vienna to Paris or from Bordeaux to Toulouse. In Lyon, they changed trains without any difficulties. Shortly after the train departed from Lyon, the French Alps began to appear in the foreground, its grey mountaintops looking like an artist's painted rendering against a brilliant blue sky.

They rode the train car mostly in silence. Alfons did his best to keep Helgi, who was now four years old, entertained by having her guess which fist was holding small pieces of candy or impersonating various animal sounds. Alfons quizzed her in fluent French, which impressed both of his parents. Other than that, there was little interaction exchanged between Alfons and his

## Chapter 25

parents. They could not imperil their hidden identities as Austrian Jews, even if their fake origins from the Alsace region would conceal their native accents.

For most of the trip, Alfons gazed out the window of the train. It was moving fast, and the glorious French mountains dared not to move in the distance. Alfons walked up and down the train aisle to stretch his legs, studying the expressions on his parents' faces. There was so much he wanted to ask his father and tell him about his own experiences during the last two years.

His father looked older and his eyes rested in sunken hallows that had formed from meager consumption in the labor camps at Gurs and Rivesaltes, but his mind continued to work in overdrive. His mother looked tired and restless, but the resourcefulness and inner strength she had demonstrated in leaving Paris and hiding him and Helgi when conditions became more perilous in the south, gave Alfons hope that they would find their way together to Switzerland.

When they arrived in Evian, they found a *dépanneur* corner store where they bought several loaves of bread and juice to fill them after fourteen hours without food or drink. Alexander bought a camera and asked the shop owner for the direction of Route D1005, which they would have to follow northeast to bring them to the Swiss border.

Occasional cars and horse-drawn carriages passed them as they walked along the side of the road. Alfons wondered if anyone else they saw were also refugees seeking asylum at the Swiss border. The road was flat, but the rugged terrain of the Alps was getting closer. After walking for about five hours with the sun setting behind them, Alexander saw a fisherman's cabin and suggested they sleep there for the night.

## Live and Be Counted

Peering inside, Alfons saw fishing nets, poles, hooks and a few life vests leaning against the back wall. In the center was a table with knives and scattered fish parts. It was abandoned for the night, but certainly would be used again when the sun rose. Trying to ignore the pungent waft of seafood, they laid out the nets on the floor as makeshift beds and positioned the life vests under their heads as pillows.

Elsa started to lull Helgi to sleep and the two of them passed out within minutes. Alfons and his father remained awake.

"I can't express how proud I am of you, Alfons," Alexander gently stroked his back. "How you took care of your sister when Mother was in the hospital. How you maintained your faith in God while you were hidden in the monastery. You were only eleven years old when you left Vienna and you've been asked to grow-up in an accelerated way no one could have predicted."

"Father, what was it like? How did you make it through?" Alfons asked. He could not fathom how deplorable the conditions in which his father was forced to live or the extent of the atrocities that the Nazis were committing.

"Son, we will talk about this another time," Alexander answered. "I'm tired, as I'm sure you are. I know there is a lot you want to tell me, and I will want to tell you, too. What matters now is that we are all together."

Alfons reluctantly closed his eyes and was awoken way too soon to a hungry and irritable Helgi with the first cracks of sun glistening off Lake Geneva. Elsa gave her a small morsel of bread that she had kept in her bag. She knew Alfons would be able to push forward with little food, though that didn't mitigate him waking up similarly hungry and irritable.

The Sperber family resumed the arduous walk as the roadside became hilly and replete with ditches, rocks and

## Chapter 25

overgrowth as they approached the Alps. They passed through Lugrin and Miellerie, small villages along the way where they were able to buy some fruit, bread and drinks.

When they reached Locum, more exhausted and ravenous than the day before, they had been walking already for more than twelve hours. There had not been many words spoken along the way in order for everyone to save their energy for the strenuous segment of the journey still to come. Alfons' mouth was parched, his lips cracking from dryness and little water. It was August, and the blaze of the sun was unforgiving at times, but Alfons reasoned to himself that it was far better to be trudging on this journey during the summer heat than during the blistery cold.

"This looks to be a ski resort and camping area in the Alps," Alfons observed. "There are several ski shops and signs for chalets just along this road."

Most of the recreational ski shops were closed well into August, but this area also attracted outdoor camping and hunting when the weather was nice. The sights and smells walking through Locum activated faraway memories in Alfons' mind from their store in Vienna and the winter vacations they took together in the Altenmartk ski area in central Austria.

Alfons wondered how people could take normal vacations in the bucolic area of Lake Geneva with the war ongoing. Probably French nobility able to escape from the conflicts and turmoil unfolding in the main cities. They could afford the diversion in the French Alps where there wasn't any German military presence.

With dirty clothes, worn shoes and looks of desperation, the Sperbers appeared anything but vacationers on a camping get-away. This quickly attracted the attention of several guides who billed themselves as part of the French Resistance to bring refugees through the Alps and to the Swiss border. Alexander spoke with one of the guides and after a few minutes of deliberation reached into his bag that contained the envelope of money and handed one of the guides a portion of Francs.

"I will be your navigator," the guide announced. "I understand you've already been walking for more than a day. Well, I'm afraid to inform that you have another eighteen hours of hiking through the mountains to arrive at the Swiss border. I will bring you a portion of the way and direct you to reach the border on your own. Your journey will be strenuous through forests and streams, difficult climbs and precarious rocks, wild animals and biting tics. This is the natural terrain of the French Alps."

The guide looked at his clients and tried to assess their physical ability to make the journey. As he scanned the four sojourners, he paused at Alfons and looked down at his arm. "Young man, is that a Cartier?"

Alfons saw the guide ogling his watch and hesitantly looked down at own wrist, willing it to disappear. He slowly tried to draw his arm behind his back, as if the guide would be fooled by such a juvenile trick.

"I forgot to mention that my fee also includes a Cartier watch," the guide said scornfully.

Alfons looked at his father, acknowledging the specialness of the gift he had given him for his *Bar Mitzvah* and kept with him all this time. His father nodded back in acquiesce and Alfons begrudgingly unlatched the leather strap from his wrist and handed the guide his watch.

The guide sneered in loathing satisfaction, the cynical joy of exploiting a desperate family, and continued as if that particular act of extortion was routine. "You'll be entering the habitat of many wild animals that may feel threatened by your presence and could attack you in defense. Also, you're going to reach higher

## Chapter 25

elevations as you climb through the Alps, so despite the August heat you're feeling now, nights can become chilly. If you're persistent, you'll arrive at the border crossing with Switzerland in two days."

Alfons knew his own strength, which had grown in muscle and stamina from the daily farm and field chores he fulfilled living in the monastery. He had more reservations about his father and mother's ability to make the journey on foot. They had been weakened from malnutrition and infection over the last few years. And his sister, who had just turned four, would need to be carried at times to help get her through the rough terrain.

"Two days?" Helgi doubted. "I can't walk for two days. Al, will you carry me?"

"Helgi, don't worry about a thing. I'll put you on my shoulders, we're not going to leave you behind."

His father and mother simultaneously looked up to Alfons. Nearly four, terribly long, unforgiving years had passed since they celebrated his eleventh birthday alongside the Danube River in Vienna with his seven pairs of aunts and uncles, and all his first cousins. He was just a normal child with ginger hair, talented at dodgeball, diligent in his school studies and interested in American cowboy films. He had developed into a precocious teenager and faced unprecedented dangers that had fortified his faith and made him stronger.

At fifteen years old, Alfons was going to lead his family through the perils of the French Alps into Switzerland. His father and mother looked at each other, then at Alfons, and smiled. They could not be prouder of the man he had become and surrendered any apprehension or ambiguity to their son's audacious courage and intrepid confidence.

### Live and Be Counted

Alfons and his parents had left so much behind each time they were forced to flee. The Cartier watch was just an item, replaceable one day in the future, just like everything else. "We have each other," Alfons declared. "Slow and steady, we'll make it through."

## Chapter 26

June 30, 2020

Eli's summer plans were irreversibly canceled. He was registered to attend sleepaway camp, but the state governor prevented camps from opening out of fear of them becoming super-spreaders of the coronavirus.

"Papa, if done right, sleepaway camps are ideal for controlling the virus, not spreading it." Eli tried to convince his great grandfather over Zoom as if he had influence to overrule the decision. "Here's how it can work: Everyone should receive a COVID-19 test before going into the camp and only those that test negative should be allowed in. Counselors shouldn't be allowed to leave and visiting day should be canceled so that there's no additional risk of exposure. That's how you can create the perfect quarantine bubble for one or two months."

"It sounds complicated to achieve, but I supposed the governor did not want to create unnecessary risk," Papa said. "It seems safer to have children remain at home. Besides, many of these camps are in remote areas that are far from a hospital. What if there was a community transmission of coronavirus in the camp, there may not be sufficient access to medical care that could support an outbreak."

"You're probably right," Eli conceded. Spending the prior summer at sleepaway camp was one of the most exciting experiences of his young life. As much as he was going to miss it, he was devising plans and projects for July and August that would help keep him occupied around the house. He had already scored a few jobs mowing lawns and running a weekly soccer clinic for several three-year-old children in the neighborhood.

"Eli," Papa said, "I want to tell you about the camp that I went to when we crossed into Switzerland."

"Was it a sleepaway camp, like the one I go to in the summer?"

"In a way, yes," Papa related. "It wasn't called a sleepaway camp. It was called a refugee camp and was set up for families running from the Nazis who had nowhere else to go. We lived in the refugee camp for two years until the end of the war. We all had to contribute to the camp to make it run, very different from the fun and comfortable atmosphere I'm sure you remember from last summer."

"Papa, how did you get across the Swiss border?"

"Once we enlisted the help of the guide, our journey took us through the French Alps. The mountains were made up of thick forests with large roots and rocks that created tripping hazards with every step. There were steep climbs that we needed the guide to pull us through and precipitous descents where we linked our arms in a human chain to keep us from falling."

Alfons paused his own reflection of the dangerous journey and turned to Eli. "Did you ever take hikes through the woods at your sleepaway camp?"

"We sure did," Eli's excitement picked up, but at the same time crested with disappointment that he would not have those experiences this summer. "The counselors tried to startle us with sightings of black bears and poisonous snakes, but their scares were fake and we never saw any animals."

## Chapter 26

"In the Alps," Papa exclaimed, "we needed to keep our eyes open for mountain animals, especially at night when it was hard to see in front of us. The guide from the French resistance only took us about four hours into the Alps before he turned around. After that, we were on own for almost two days. We tried to go as far as we could during daylight hours since it was too difficult to walk in the dark. Father, Mother and I took shifts at night while the others slept to look out for wild animals or any other type of threat. It was August, but it became chilly during the two nights we slept on the ground in the Alps. We had no blankets or pillows, we huddled close to keep each other warm."

"How did Helgi make it through? Wasn't she around four years old?" Eli asked.

"It was almost as if she registered the gravity of the situation and went entirely with the flow. She was young, but she handled these two days in the mountains as best as anyone could have expected. I carried her on my shoulders when I could and that allowed us to move swiftly."

Papa continued, "Some parts of the journey seemed endless, surrounded by trees, rocks and sounds of nature. There was a vague path that was forming by refugees who must have been going through the Alps before us and, where they were visible, we used those tracks to guide our way."

"What did you eat and drink?" Eli wondered aloud.

"We bought some bread and fruits in Morzine, which was the last town on the French side of the border that we passed through," Papa said. "We picked berries along the way and drank water from a stream that we crossed over by forming the shape of a cup with our hands. We were hungry, for sure, but at least we had something. I ate as little as possible so my sister would have more. We needed to keep up our pace and that was going to be more easily achieved if she was eating. I kept my hunger to myself, and I'm sure Mother and Father did the same."

Eli remembered his hike in the woods with his bunk. They had energized beforehand with a large breakfast of bagels, eggs, milk and cereal and concluded the hike just a few hours later with a cookout replete with hamburgers, hotdogs, baked beans and soda. He knew it wasn't fair to compare their experiences, but it was the closest scenario he had to relate to Papa's two-day journey through the mountains.

"The trail through the mountains took us down perilous rocky slopes as well. Closer to the border, the terrain transitioned into desolate land that was filled with manure and human defecation, probably the location of where much of the sewer waste from both countries was being piped. We trudged through septic discharge and eventually arrived at a stone wall that was low to the ground."

Papa described what he had seen when they arrived at the border. "The word *FRANCE* was painted in large block letters on the side of the stone barrier we were facing. The word *SCHWEIZ* was similarly painted in block letters on the other side. After two days, exhausted, dirty, hungry and thirsty, we arrived at the Swiss border around noon."

Eli had heard on the news during the early weeks of COVID-19 that the United States was closing its borders to prevent further spread of the virus from more infectious parts of the world. He imagined the border being a towering wall with a locked gate and security guards that would prevent people from passing through without approval. "What was the border between France and Switzerland like?"

"It was a simple barrier about one meter high that was made of large stones. There was no one monitoring the wall or

## Chapter 26

anyone in sight. We gingerly climbed over, looking for guards or soldiers, but there was just more trees and forest ahead. We made it to Switzerland, but we still were in the middle of nowhere."

Eli had traveled with his parents and siblings through various states across America during summer and winter vacations. He started to fathom how states and countries protected their borders. In the US, there were often bridges, tolls or simply large welcome signs on the highway that separated one state from another. For the most part, one could pass freely.

He wondered what it was like to pass from the US to Mexico in the south or to Canada in the north. Were there border fences or walls that physically separated the territories from each other? Were they guarded by border policemen or soldiers to prevent illegal migrants from coming in? Perhaps they were equipped with electronic sensors that could be monitored remotely.

"Switzerland bordered with France to the west, Germany to the north, Austria to the east and Italy to the south," Papa explained. "There were times during the war that Switzerland refused to let Jewish refugees in, claiming that there was dwindling supplies. Records show that twenty-seven thousand Jews crossed into Switzerland for asylum during the war, but it's estimated that thousands were also turned away or sent back."

"Since Switzerland also bordered Austria, did your family think about escaping to Switzerland rather than going to France?" Eli asked.

"Remember that my father had contacts in Paris, and he was strategically setting up a business and a home for us where we could live, not just abscond," Papa said. "We could not have known at the time that the Germans would occupy France, as well as Belgium, Luxembourg and Holland, after they annexed Austria.

## Live and Be Counted

Many Jews from Austria did in fact try to enter Switzerland in 1938, but the Nazis were marking the passports of German and Austrian Jews with a special *J* stamp. The Swiss, wanting to appease the Germans with their neutrality, let in tourists and other foreigners, but turned away Jews."

"Why did Germany not invade Switzerland like they did many of the other countries in Europe?" Eli inquired.

Alfons had done a great deal of reading on World War Two as details of the Holocaust emerged and were published after his arrival in America. "Germany agreed not to occupy to Switzerland if they could use Swiss banks to hide gold, art and money that was pilfered from Jewish homes and businesses. Another theory was that Switzerland agreed with Hitler to provide refuge to Nazi war criminals in case of their defeat. Germany was more threatened by a potential counter-attack from England and the United States on the western front and probably did not want to thin its military by occupying a landlocked country such as Switzerland."

Eli was getting quite a lesson in history and geography. His Risk game board did not demarcate the country lines that Papa was describing. Territories were grouped more simply into Northern Europe, Western Europe and Southern Europe. While Papa was talking, Eli switched his screen to Google Maps and opened a browser that showed the country lines of current day Europe. The visualization made him better appreciate the distances his great grandfather had to travel.

"Switzerland loosened their borders to foreigners in 1941 and 1942, while Germany was focusing their efforts on the occupation in northern France. When Germany completed their occupation of southern France in November of 1942, Switzerland tightened their borders once again."

## Chapter 26

"And you were fleeing from southern France, right?" Eli remarked.

"Yes, we were. In August 1942 we got across the border from France to Switzerland just in time."

## Chapter 27

August 1942

Alfons, along with his parents and sister, continued lumbering through the woods. Several hours after crossing to the Swiss side of the border, the dense forest on the French side began to part into open fields and rolling hills. It was getting dark and a refreshing chill came sweeping across the high altitude to alleviate the uncomfortable humidity that beset them during the day.

They set their eyes on the smokestacks of a factory up ahead. The closer they got, the stronger they could scent a sweet aroma permeating through the air. It was hard to detect what they were smelling, but whatever it was, it was comforting and inviting.

Suddenly Helgi cried out, "Cheese! I smell cheese!"

"She's right!" Alfons followed, as the aroma evoked memories of his own. "We made cheese on the farm at the monastery. That must be a cheese factory up ahead."

"Maybe they will let us sleep there for the night, before we continue toward the refugee camp," Elsa offered.

The actual factory consisted of a long, rectangular single-story building with a simple A-shaped roof and several smokestacks on the north side. The factory was surrounded by grazing pastures, set in a valley between two hills in the Alps. There were several large, red barns in the pasture and a quaint cottage with a wrap-around porch on the far end of the grounds. Most of the lights in the cottage were on, which was not surprising since it was early evening.

## Chapter 27

"They must be having dinner now," Alexander said. "We've been on our feet for almost three days. We're exhausted, hungry and thirsty. Let's knock on the door, we have nothing to lose."

Alexander walked up the steps to the porch and knocked three times. Within a few moments, a man opened the door wearing blue coveralls, a beige hat and brown boots. Alfons surveyed the man and reasoned he was probably in his mid-forties, the same age as his father. The man presented with broad shoulders, a square chin and towering frame, very much in contrast to how Alexander had aged during the two years he was interned at Gurs and Rivesaltes.

"I'm scared, Al. Is he a nice man?" Helgi scurried behind her brother and poked her head cautiously around his leg, intimidated by the copious size of the man at the door.

"Don't worry Helgi. Father will speak to him," Alfons comforted her.

Alexander cleared his throat. "Please forgive us for interrupting your dinner. The war is worsening in France and we were shown the way through the Alps to Switzerland. We're headed to the Aigle until it's safe to return to France. Please can you show us the way?"

The man in the blue coveralls placed his hands on his hips and let out an exuberant laugh. Two of his children heard his laugh and scurried to the door to see what the commotion was about. "I am a God-fearing Catholic and know that the Lord has put me in this cheese factory near the French border for a reason. You and your family will eat with us tonight and sleep in the barn. Tomorrow morning we'll pack up some food and send you on your way to Aigle."

## Live and Be Counted

Alfons wondered if they were the first refugees to knock on their door, especially if other Jews had followed a similar route across the Swiss border as they had.

"We appreciate your kindness and God will repay you tenfold for your hospitality," Alexander said accepting the gracious invitation.

The man in blue coveralls stuck out his hand, "The name's Chezmann, Leon Chezmann. Farm's been in the family for four generations. Been living here forty-five years since I was born, never left the farm." Alexander took his hand and winced at the strength of Leon's grip over his.

The Sperbers joined the Chezmann's for dinner, consisting of vegetable cheese soufflé with potatoes, bread and milk. They were famished after three days in the Alps, rationing whatever meager food they took with them and whatever berries they foraged along the way. After dinner, they were treated to a tour of the factory.

"We take pride in our cheese," Leon proclaimed on the guided tour, still wearing the blue coveralls. "Swiss cheese flavor is sweet and nut-like, known for being shiny, pale yellow in color. It gets rolled onto one-hundred-kilogram wheels before it is thinned and sliced."

He turned to Alfons and said, "Young man, I'll bet you're wondering how Swiss cheese gets its eyes."

"You mean the holes in the cheese, sir?" Alfons tried to show his excitement for the cheese tour, but was exhausted from the last few days and ready to crash for the night.

"Well, those large holes aren't made from mice who eat through them. No, that's just an old wives' tale!" Leon humored himself with a joke he had probably told countless of times.

## Chapter 27

"Swiss cheese gets its distinctive holes from bacteria mixed with cow's milk. The cheese is heated and cooled multiple times throughout the process, causing the bacteria to expand and release carbon dioxide, which creates all of those eyes that make Swiss cheese famous."

"I definitely didn't know that," Alfons nodded his head as if the cheese making process all made sense to him now.

"I'll also bet you didn't know that Swiss cheese is known for being among the healthiest of cheeses. It's an excellent source of protein and calcium and contains more vitamin B than other cheeses, making it a great choice for a balanced diet."

Alfons reckoned that Mr. Chezmann was also a natural cheese salesman.

"Here," Leon Chezmann extended his hand to each of the Sperbers with large wedges of Swiss cheese he took from inside an industrial refrigerator. "Help yourself and enjoy."

Helgi was the first to take a bite and she shrieked with joy over its sweetness. "This is yummy," she exclaimed and put out her hand for a second helping before she even finished the first wedge. Everyone laughed at her brashness, which succeeded in landing her an extra piece of cheese.

Their host was proud of the factory that had been part of his family for over one hundred years, but admitted that sales to distributors in France and Germany had declined sharply since the war. Businesses all around were suffering with rationing currencies, inflationary pressure and unemployment. "Exports just aren't what they used to be, which is where we generate most of our revenue," Leon explained. "We've had to scale back some our production as consumer demand and purchasing power for delicacies dry up."

## Live and Be Counted

Alexander added, "I used to own a factory as well, sports clothing and coats. It was very successful with distribution across Austria, Germany and France. The Germans took it from me in 1938."

"I'll bet your coats did not smell as good as my cheese!" Leon ribbed Alexander with his elbow and Alexander moved his own hands to sooth the spot from his jabbing. "Tomorrow, I go into town to make deliveries to local stores. You can all ride in my truck and I'll bring you to the train station that will take you to Aigle."

Alexander thanked him as Leon brought them to a barn full of hay and farm animals. For Alfons, the inside of the barn conjured recollections from the night they slept in a barn on the way to Bordeaux. There was a stack of folded blankets at the back of the barn and Alfons wondered if other refugees had been allowed to sleep here. The weather was mild, but the blankets gave them warmth and comfort.

As the rest of family fell into a restless sleep, Alfons lay awake. So much had happened over the past four years, it was becoming harder for him to retrace all the steps they had each taken since leaving Vienna.

Alfons could see his father turn over two or three times to get more comfortable, struggling to fall asleep. "Father," Alfons whispered, not wanting to wake Helgi or his mother. "Please tell me what it was like? How did the Nazis treat you?"

Alexander again deflected the question. "Alfons, I promise we will talk about this another time and I'll share my stories with you. For now, my son, I am tired and want to sleep."

"Father, please anything. I need to know about the atrocities. I was hidden away for almost a year and half. I came out from hiding in the monastery and the war is still going on. You

## Chapter 27

were imprisoned in a Nazi camp for two years and I want to know how they treated you."

Alexander let up his guard and relented for just a little bit. He knew that Alfons had grown up quicker than most children needed to and faced challenges equally as daring. Alexander decided that his son had earned the right to hear what he had gone through. "For all the time I was in the labor camp, I was a prisoner. I was mostly used to sledgehammer large rocks into limestone, which were probably used to build fortifications for Nazis on the frontlines. The work was backbreaking, but I needed to be productive and remain useful in order to stay alive."

Alexander paused for a moment to reflect. "There was a man named Julius who slept next to me in the barracks."

Alfons held his breath, clinging onto every word.

"Julius was interned for hard labor with me in Rivesaltes and his wife Rose worked in the camp's kitchen. They were in their mid-forties, around my age. Julius and Rose fled Germany in 1939 to Holland with their two children just as conditions were becoming perilous for German Jews. I think their children's names were Richard and Clare, but I don't remember exactly. When the Germans invaded Holland in 1940, they arrested many Jews, especially those that had fled from the Nazis in Germany. Julius and Rose were forced to leave their children behind with friends who lived in The Hague where they were hidden in the attic. After their arrest, Julius and Rose were sent by the Nazis to Rivesaltes, the same camp in which I was imprisoned."

Alfons immediately felt the similarity with his own experiences, hearing how these parents also had to hide their children.

"After just a few weeks in the camp, Julius was severely weakened from dehydration and lack of food. I feared that if he

## Live and Be Counted

could not fulfill his limestone quotas, the Nazis would render him useless and kill him. One time when Julius was resting on the side to ward off dizziness and nausea, a Nazi guard hit him in the back of the head with the butt of his rifle, knocking him bloodily to the ground."

This nightmarish glimpse into the labor camp conditions frightened Alfons. He wondered if his father endured physical beatings as well.

"That night, as the lights in the barracks were shut off, I turned over to Julius who slept in the cot next to mine and told him that his wife Rose should inform the guards that she was pregnant and needed to seek a doctor to terminate the pregnancy rather than give birth to a baby in the camp. If they would be granted permission to visit a doctor in the city, perhaps they could maneuver an escape to the south and cross into Spain until the war was over."

"Father, what happened to them? Did they escape?" Alfons asked, still holding onto every word of the story.

"Julius was initially apprehensive about this idea and it took several nights of convincing that there was no better option if he was seeking a way to escape. Later that week, he mustered enough courage to make the request with the guards. A few days later, Julius and Rose were taken together in a military jeep out of the camp, but I never saw them return and will likely never see them again. I don't know what happened to them, but I pray to God that Julius and Rose found their way to Spain."

As Alfons' eyelids got heavier and began to envelop him in an exhaustive sleep, he wondered if his father's friends found the border with Spain and were still alive. Alexander still didn't talk about how he was personally treated by the Nazis, but Alfons was heartened to hear about his father's cleverness and the way he

## Chapter 27

looked out after others like Julius and Rose in the labor camp, even when conditions endangered his own wellbeing.

When the sun rose the next morning, the Sperbers joined the Chezmann family for breakfast with a spread that included milk, eggs, toast and an assortment of cheeses. They packed some of the extras for lunch and piled into the truck for a thirty-minute ride into the town of Champery, where Leon dropped them at the train station.

The Swiss officers at the station gave the Sperbers leery looks while they inspected their French identifications at the ticket counter. This process sent pulses of nerves through Alfons' body, not that dissimilar from those he experienced leaving Vienna, Paris and Bordeaux. Once again, their lives depended on admission, or at least non-suspicion, for the next leg of their journey.

"You may board the train," a policeman declared after stamping their papers, letting Alfons release a sigh of relief. "You will take the train five stops to Aigle and from there a policeman will direct you to the camp."

Unlike the Gare du Nord in Paris, there was only one platform to choose from. Champery was the first stop on the local line and the Sperbers boarded the Swiss train, carrying only the backpacks with which they started their journey four days earlier in Toulouse.

Elsa inspected the inside of her backpack for the gold jewelry tucked at the bottom, a motion Alfons noted had become a habit since leaving Vienna. The jewelry was valuable, but more poignantly it was one of the few tangible possessions that Elsa had left which allowed her to feel connected to her life before the war. It brought her back to a milieu of comfort and prestige which was stolen from her by the Nazis.

## Live and Be Counted

As the train pulled away from the station, Elsa cupped her palms around Alfons' hands. "If I lose the gold jewelry, so be it. I have you, I have Helgi and the three of us have your father. The Nazis cannot touch our memories or the happy moments we shaped together as a family in Vienna."

Alfons looked crestfallen. "I wasn't ready to just have memories. We had our home, we had our friends, we had our aunts, uncles and cousins. I had Ludwig." Alfons felt bad that he hadn't thought about his best friend in a while and continued to wonder whether his family had escaped from Austria, like he did, or had been deported to Dachau.

"I know dear, I know. I feel the same way," his mother tried to comfort him. "When the four of us were hiding or imprisoned all in different places, I did not know if we'd ever reunite. I never gave up hope and I prayed to God each day that we could be a family again."

"What will it be like when we get to the refugee camp?" Alfons asked.

His father entered the conversation. "This Swiss government designated several refugee camps near the French border giving asylum to Jews and non-Jews who have fled because of the war," Alexander explained. "We'll have to wait and see what it will be like."

"What will I do while we're there?" Alfons asked.

"I'm not sure, but we'll want to make ourselves useful as much as possible while we're in the camp. It will keep us motivated and accepted if we need to stay there for a long period of time." This response satisfied Alfons, since after all, contributing to the communal needs was a tenant of monastery living.

## Chapter 27

They arrived in Aigle after a twenty-five-minute train ride and, after stepping onto the platform, a policeman asked to see their papers again. Accepting of their identifications, he directed the Sperbers to a road that was a thirty-minute walk to the Aigle ski lodge.

Nestled in the mountains of the Swiss Alps, Aigle was a popular ski chalet before the main lodge was repurposed as a haven for asylum seekers. The main lodge with its sleeping rooms usually reserved for vacationers was situated on a hill dotted with large pine trees and untamed grass.

"The Swiss government took over the Aigle ski lodge several months ago," Alexander explained to Alfons. "As a neutral country in the war, Switzerland has been receiving pressure from the United States and other countries to take in refugees."

When the Sperbers registered at Aigle, Swiss officials at the camp informed them their stay would be temporary until they could be permanently placed at another site. Aigle was a staging camp so that the Swiss government could organize migrants from France to various other camps that were being established. Their notice came two weeks after arriving in Aigle that they would be transferred to Morgins, another ski motel seconded by the Swiss government to deal with the refugees.

"Father, isn't Morgins back near the French border?" Alfons asked remembering the map he had studied along the foot journey through the Alps.

"Yes, I think it is," he responded. "Why do you ask?"

"I'm just thinking that sending us back near the French border is purposeful," Alfons deduced. "This way, if the Germans come for us, they won't have to go deep into Swiss territory."

### Live and Be Counted

"I shudder to think about it, my son," Alexander said. "Morgins is our final hope. There is nowhere left to go."

# Chapter 28

July 15, 2020

"Eli, have you ever gone skiing before?" Papa asked at the start of their Zoom session.

It had been a few weeks since Alfons and Eli had last spoken. The warm weather of summer was drawing Eli outside to the backyard and he was filling his time riding bicycles with friends, teaching one-on-one soccer skills to neighborhood youths and mowing lawns of newcomers who were fleeing the city and craving suburban space from the extended lockdowns. Outdoor activities that could safely meet social distancing requirements.

Alfons was glad to still have Eli's attention. He was nearing the end of his story and there were still stories from his personal memoir he wanted to share.

"Skiing?" Eli asked incredulously. "Papa, you know it's the middle of the summer!"

"Of course, it's the middle of the summer!" Papa laughed. "Skiing happens in the winter when the snow comes! So tell me, do you go skiing?"

"We sure do, Papa," Eli answered. "My father took us last year to learn how to ski and sometimes I go snow tubing with my school. I'll bet skiing would also be a good social distancing activity. It's outdoors and there's plenty of space between the chairs on the ski lift."

"Would you believe me if I told you that I used to go skiing all the time? I was actually quite good!" Papa drew from the tucked-away winter getaways he took with his parents in the Austrian mountains before the war. Ski pants were a popular item in his father's store. At the refugee camp, he made the best with what he had to enjoy the slopes.

Alfons explained how Morgins was surrounded by large pine trees with several ski trails that converged at the bottom near the main lodge, a three-story, three-sided building with more than one hundred guest rooms and an eating hall.

"This sounds more like a resort than a refugee camp," Eli imagined a full array of amenities at the ski lodge Papa was describing.

"Oh, it was nothing like a resort that you picture today. When we arrived in September 1942, the Swiss government had converted the Morgins ski motel into an internment camp for Jewish refugees. There were rooms like you would find in a motel, but there were no services or comforts. In fact, living space was very tight and we all had communal roles."

Alfons figured there were close to five hundred Jewish refugees who, like him, had reached Morgins by crossing over the Alps from eastern France. Morgins became known as the *Alpine Shtetl*, a reference to the small towns in Germany, Austria and Poland where Jewish families lived tightly, celebrating the holidays together and performing the traditions as a community.

Switzerland's Jewish communities in Zurich, Geneva and Basel, which were not immediately threatened from Nazi occupation, formed the Swiss Aid Society to organize donations for Morgins and other refugee camps. Volunteers brought clothing, kosher meats, medications, books and toys to help create a sense of normalcy in a temporary situation that no one knew how long would last.

## Chapter 28

"All the adults took on responsibilities to run the camp," Papa explained. "Mother taught in the kindergarten they had formed while Father worked as a cook in the kitchen and led *Torah* study groups and prayer services. Everyone worked hard six days a week so that we could enjoy *Shabbat* together in song, prayer and relaxation."

Alfons thought about how well his sister, who was four years old at the time, fit in the kindergarten with the other boys and girls around her age. Eli saw a grin crawl across Papa's face as he looked away from the camera. "Helgi spoke French to some and German to others, but most of the time she confused the two languages entirely!"

"What about you, Papa? How did you adjust to the camp?"

"I was fifteen years old when we arrived at Morgins, and the nursery and kindergarten were for younger children. I spent days in the forest collecting wood that was needed for cooking food and heating fireplaces. I also helped my father in the kitchen preparing meals and cleaning up. Twice a day I hiked to a farm eight kilometers each way to buy milk, each time hauling twenty-five liters in two large jugs tied to a wooden pole across my shoulders."

Eli felt bad for Papa, who experienced a childhood spent running, hiding and working. He knew the lockdown challenges brought upon by the coronavirus paled in comparison.

"I had my moments of enjoyment, too. Remember I asked you earlier if you liked to go skiing?"

Eli nodded yes.

"When the first snow fell in January 1943, I had already discovered the storage room at Morgins where they kept all of the ski equipment. Eli, do you know what skis were made of back then?" Papa asked.

This time Eli nodded no.

"Today, skis are made of hard fiberglass that are very sturdy and lock in securely with ski boots," Papa explained. "When I was your age, skis were actually made from wood!" He described how buckled straps were used to secure their shoes to the skis. "Those shoes didn't quite keep our feet warm like snow boots today. We had to wear multiple layers of socks, and often that wasn't enough!"

"The day that it snowed, I took a pair of skis from the storage room and spent over two hours hiking up the mountain. The chairs from the ski lift dangled inoperably above me fifty feet off the ground. I could barely feel my toes and fingers by the time I reached the top. I took a deep breath and let the adrenaline kick in as I raced down."

"Go, Papa!" Eli cheered him on.

"I went up and down the slope again and again." Alfons stepped away from the iPad for a few minutes and returned with a photograph. "One of the times down the slope, my parents and Helgi were at the bottom having their own fun in the snow, building snowmen and forts. Father brought out his Kodak Vigilant Junior Six-20 folding camera and captured the moment." He positioned the

## Chapter 28

photo in the center of the iPad frame so that Eli could see it. Alfons marveled at the photo himself, a rare jewel of their life during the war, that his father kept with him during their journey to America.

"At the end of the day, I was so tired and frostbitten that I collapsed on my bed in exhaustion and didn't wake up until after lunch the next day!"

With so much tragedy in his wake, Alfons had consolidated mostly the positive memories from his experiences in the Holocaust. Skiing in the Swiss Alps provided a sense undiluted childhood fun when there was otherwise little to no reservoir of normalcy to draw from. In the Morgins refugee camp, where the geographic buffer of Switzerland kept them largely out of reach from the Nazi genocide occurring throughout the rest of Europe, Alfons was among the fortunate ones that made it through with his immediately family intact. Retelling aspects of his personal story that ran contrary to the experiences of those who lived through the concentration camps and witnessed the murder of their families had sheathed him with survivor's guilt.

Yet, as much as Morgins offered Jewish refugees temporary safety, the Swiss themselves lived under constant political and military threats from the Germans. The Luftwaffe violated Swiss airspace more than five hundred times between 1942 and 1945, running missions aimed at deterring a counterattack by the Allied Forces from Italy, which bordered Switzerland on the south. Occasionally, German aircraft lightly punished the Swiss from above for not fortifying their borders and allowing a small flow Jewish and other asylum seekers into the country.

The German Luftwaffe successfully served to intimidate the Swiss from entering the war. As a result, it was an easy target for the Swiss to blame Jewish refugees as the reason for Europe's second war in twenty-five years. They were Nazi sympathizers living in Switzerland just as there were in France.

Every few weeks, Alexander would lead groups of fifteen or twenty people from the camp into the local town to buy supplies and medicines. These hikes to and from the retail district of Morgins took a full day by and usually were uneventful. "One of our ventures into town came just a day after a Nazi air intrusion and the shop owners and residents were particularly on edge when our group arrived."

Like some of Papa's stories before this, Eli had a premonition that something ominous was going to happen, a stark reminder that his great grandfather's childhood was anything but normal. He waited while Papa organized his memories.

Eli heard Papa retell how his group dispersed among the various cafes, shops and stores and met back up in front of the drug store to start their hike back to the camp. "Father began to lead the group and I floated toward the rear of the group to make sure no one was left behind. As we moved forward, a Swiss policeman emerged from the drug store near where I was standing and aimed his rifle toward the front of the group. *'Heil Hitler!'* he shouted without warning in a German dialect and squeezed the trigger. The shot from his rifle shattered the tranquility in the village and sent Father and others scampering to the ground."

"Oh my!" Eli cried. "Was anyone hit?"

"Fortunately, the first shot missed. But the policeman took aim a second time. As he pulled the trigger, I lunged at his hands and forced the gun upward to the sky as the bullet emerged. I was blinded by the radiant sun shining directly in my eyes and became dizzy from the sharp odor of the gun powder that singed my nose. Then suddenly everything went dark."

Eli's heart was racing.

## Chapter 28

"When I opened my eyes many minutes later, my nose singed with another sharp smell, this time of rubbing alcohol. The sun with still shining brightly, casting a large shadow of my father behind him as he slowly came into focus. He was hovering over me, waving smelling salts underneath my nose."

"Papa, what happened to you?"

"After I pushed the gun's direction from the policeman's hands away from the group, the policeman hit me on the back of the head with the butt of the gun and knocked me unconscious. My head pounded for days and, looking back, I probably had suffered a concussion from the blunt force."

"Papa, you saved your friends! You saved your father!"

"Father later told me that two other Swiss policemen ran to the scene and tackled the first policeman that fired at us."

"Papa, this was the second time you were shot and almost killed. On your way to Bordeaux, you dove beneath the carriage and acted as a shield between the bullets and your sister. In Switzerland, you risked your life to jump in front of the Swiss policeman when he shot his gun. You never hesitated. I know you owe your life to so many others, but there are just as many people who owe their lives to you."

"I never thought about it that way," Papa said. "I just acted."

As they ended their Zoom call, Alfons smiled. He never looked for recognition or expected to be thanked. His whole life, he always tried to put others before himself. He always tried to make a difference in other people's lives.

He tried to live the Abbot's blessing to him, and that of Moses to Reuven before him.

# Chapter 29

May 1943

It had been nine months since arriving at Morgins, and with the war ongoing, there was no indication when they would be able to return home. More Jewish families continued to arrive and the Swiss authorities largely left the refugees on their own. Alfons was serving the camp gathering firewood, hauling milk and helping in the kitchen, but he longed to be in school with other teenagers.

A social worker sent by the Swiss Aid Society came to the camp for a few days each month to check on the welfare of the inhabitants. Her visits served to replenish medications and other necessary supplies. On one of her visits, she met with the Sperbers.

"Alfons, you're quite tall for your age. I see that you are sixteen, but I could have mistaken you for grown adult!" the social worker jested. It wasn't the first time Alfons was thought by others to be older than he was. It didn't bother him, but there were moments he wanted to go back to being a regular teenager. War had forced him to grow up much quicker.

"I should be in tenth grade, but I don't think I'll ever have the chance to go back to school," Alfons said despondently.

With a sense of belated remorse, Elsa and Alexander looked at each other. It was one of the few times in the last several years that Alfons ever expressed his own personal desires, even as subtly as he just had.

"I know, dear," his mother emphasized, "but there's not much we can do about it. It's beyond our control."

## Chapter 29

"It may not be out of your control," the social worker suggested. "We have been placing some teenagers from other refugee camps with Swiss families to work farms and be nannies for their hosts." Turning to Alfons she said promisingly, "Maybe we can foster you at a family where you can also go to school during the day."

Alfons' eyes lit up, but only momentarily, having never considered what it would be like to leave the camp and return to school. Hesitantly he answered, "I'm not sure if it would be a good idea to leave my parents."

"Alfons, let's hear more what the social worker has to say," his father said encouragingly, warming up to the idea himself.

"Well, there are families who need older boys and girls to help in their homes and with their businesses," the social worker explained. "In exchange, they provide a place to live and eat. Sometimes work is needed in the morning or at night, so perhaps we can find a family where you can also attend school."

This option was starting to sound attractive to Alfons, but he didn't want to appear too eager. He was still torn about leaving his parents and sister, and wasn't sure how far away he would be fostered or how often he would be able to see them.

Alexander saw the hesitation in Alfons' expression. "Son, we're safe here in Morgins," he reassured him, as only a father could. "Switzerland will remain neutral in the war and the Nazis are not crossing the border. If you have the opportunity to return to high school, you have our full support. The *Talmud* teaches us that a wise person is one who learns from every person. Go, Alfons. Finish your schooling."

"We'll make arrangements for you to return to Morgins for the Jewish holidays," his mother added. "Don't worry about us, we will be fine here."

### Live and Be Counted

Alfons turned to the social worker and nodded in ascent, but with a heavy heart. He completed an application form and within a few weeks learned that he would be fostered by a family with five children in Pfaeffikon, a village outside of Zurich about 270 kilometers from Morgins. The next month, Mr. Walder arrived at the camp in his 1936 blue Opel Kadett to meet Alfons and bring him back to Pfaeffikon.

Saying goodbye to his parents and sister once again wasn't easy, but it was more heartening to know there was a sense of tranquility and calm in the refugee camp. Alexander helped Alfons bring his suitcases to the car.

"Son, the family that is fostering you is not Jewish. You'll be able to come back to the Morgins camp for the holidays, but you'll find it difficult to observe our traditions while you're living with the Walders. Do your best, but don't try to do it all. When the war is over, we'll bring back our observances together."

"Father, I didn't tell you this, but while I was living in the monastery, I wore my *t'fillin* each day and I never ate meat that wasn't kosher. Being in an environment that was devoid of Jewish rituals strengthened my faith. You don't need to worry about me while I'm in Pfaeffikon."

Alexander put his arms around Alfons a second time. "I could not be any prouder of you, my son." He moved his hands to the top of Alfons head in an act he had repeated each Friday night as the Sperbers welcomed the start of the *Shabbat* while they lived in Vienna. He then recited the ancient priestly blessing which Jewish fathers have had the tradition of delivering to their children for more than two thousand years. With tears welling in his eyes, he kissed Alfons' forehead and beseeched, "May God bless you and watch over you."

## Chapter 29

Elsa approach Alfons and repeated the same gesture, reaching her hands upward atop his head and completed the blessing. "May God be gracious to you and give you peace."

Helgi walked over to her older brother and held his hand. "I don't want you to go," she grimaced. "Who will be my big brother? Who will look after me?"

Alfons threw Helgi up into the air, eliciting a shriek of joy from the five-year-old girl, and catching her cleanly on the way down. He bent down until he was eye-level with his sister and held both of her hands. "Helgi, I will always be your big brother," he promised her. "Even when you are all grown up and have your own family, I'll always be your big brother." He squeezed her tight and felt his own eyes grow heavy with teardrops, trying to wipe them away so that no one would see.

"I miss you already," Helgi hugged him back, wrapping her arms around his neck and kissing him on the cheek.

Alfons stood up and loaded his suitcase with clothing he had received as donations from the Swiss Aid Society into the trunk of Mr. Walder's car. This wasn't the first time he was going to live separately from his family, but Mr. Walder vowed to Alfons that he'd be part of the family, not forced to live in hiding or under a false identity.

From the backseat of the car, Alfons turned to look out the rear window as it drove away down the road. He could not shed himself from the guilt of leaving his family behind. He waved until his parents and sister were mere fragments of the Morgins refugee camp in the distance. Agonizing memories flashed through his mind, the same nightmares that often woke him in the middle of the night in the monastery.

## Live and Be Counted

Tearful memories of the ghastly fear he felt when Ludwig Manheim and his family disappeared, possibly having been sent to their deaths at Dachau.

Frightful memories of hiding behind the cash register while his father was brutalized by the Nazis in their store and their narrow escape from Austria to Paris.

Traumatic memories of sleeping in mosquito-ridden barns on the side of the road to Bordeaux and shielding his baby sister from the lethal bullets hissing through the air from the German Luftwaffe.

Painful memories of not knowing whether his mother would recover from her infection and reliving the piercing screams as Alice Resch took Helgi to the orphanage.

Dreadful memories of the infinite loneliness he felt when he was handed a set of brown robes at the monastery, living in constant fear that he would be discovered.

Awful memories of hunger and thirst he endured for three days climbing across the border through the French Alps.

The car motored forward and Alfons prayed to God to keep his family safe in the refugee camp. He took temporary solace knowing that his mother and sister were together under the protective wing of his father. The three people who mattered most in his life would look after each other. Alfons' conviction remained strong, despite profound tests of faith he had endured.

Alfons would later reckon that the small prayer he offered in Mr. Walder's car went straight to the ears of God. There were many reasons to question why God was allowing the massacre of so many people and allowing such indescribable suffering. It's not that Alfons did not have these questions, he did. He was simply

## Chapter 29

offering a prayer requesting that God continue to look after him and his family. He did not know how to ask for anything more.

Alfons would look back on that car ride and know definitively that God had answered his small prayer. Back at the refugee camp, Alfons later learned that his sister Helgi was playing with another boy on the swings when they both saw a pair of long-winged, front propeller planes cutting down from the clouds above them.

Looking up, frozen in fear at the sight of the two planes roaring toward them, the young boy shouted. "Run Helgi! Run!" The two young children jumped off the swings, scurrying as fast as they could toward the dining hall, which was the shelter closest to them. Inside, Alexander and several others were cleaning up from lunch.

Just as Helgi's father turned to hear the shattering cries from the terrified girl, a quick sequence of explosions shook the building and knocked them all to the ground. The two children lay motionless under Alexander's protective arm until the sound of the planes was gone and could be reasonably certain they were not returning for a second strike.

The others in the dining hall who also dove for coverage signaled to each other that it seemed safe to come out, cautiously creeping toward the entrance and poking their heads outside to survey the damage that the German bombs had caused. Children and adults across the main areas of the camp warily came out from their hiding places too.

Everything looked intact. There didn't seem to be anything in the camp that was hit by the bombs. Then Helgi saw the smoke plumes in the distance. "Look, Father," she pointed to a cow field about five hundred meters beyond the barbed wire fence that demarcated the grounds of the camp. Dirt and dust that was awoken from the bombs was settling back to the earth. Smoke rising from the ground was dissipating into the air. "The planes missed us, Father! They hit the poor cows instead! Oh, those poor cows."

Driving onward in the car with Mr. Walder, Alfons covered his eyes and recited *Shema Yisrael* in his heart, a prayer taught to every Jewish boy and girl at a young age. "Keep my family safe, Oh God of Israel. Keep my family safe."

# Chapter 30

June 1943 - May 1945

"Alfons, you're going to fit right in with us," Mr. Walder assured him during the four-hour drive from Morgins to Pfaeffikon. "We're going to need your help on the farm and in our bakery. We have five children, but they are younger than you and can't be relied on fully to help us with all of the chores and responsibilities."

"Thank you, Mr. Walder," Alfons responded back to him with confidence and a bit of excitement. "I had to work on a farm in France, so I'm ready to help do what's needed. Will I also be going to school in Pfaeffikon?"

"You will, young man. There is a public high school in the town next door where you'll be able to resume your studies in math, science and history."

"I don't think I can count on two hands how many different schools I've been to over the past five years." Alfons used his pointer to tap each one of his fingers in a counting whisper starting with the Stern Yeshiva and the Gymnasium in Vienna. He included the middle school in Paris and the afternoon Hebrew school that supplemented his general studies. In Toulouse, he attended a school before going into hiding in the monastery, which he also included in his count from the nightly lessons he had with the Abbot.

Alfons yearned to be back in a classroom.

When they arrived at the Walder's farm, five children stumbled out of the house to greet their newly adopted brother.

## Live and Be Counted

The children were followed by a woman that Alfons presumed was Mrs. Walder.

"Meet Urli, Ruth, Erica, Margaret and Jack," Mr. Walder announced proudly. The children, whose ages ranged from fifteen to two years, each put out their hands in unison to extend their greetings to Alfons. "And of course the backbone of our family, Mrs. Walder."

"It's a pleasure to meet you Alfons," Mrs. Walder was carrying a tray of freshly baked chocolate chip cookies. The steam from the cookies was still rising into the air. "Welcome. We've been looking forward to your arrival for a few weeks. You're going to be very comfortable living here and we want you to be part of the family." The Walders spoke a Swiss German dialect which made it easy for Alfons to converse in his native tongue.

"Thank you everyone," Alfons returned the greeting and shook each of the children's hands that had been extended to him. "I'm very grateful to be here and want to help out in any way that I can. Switzerland is a beautiful country and my drive with Mr. Walder was really the first time seeing the countryside away from the French border."

"Oh, we've got plenty of work for you here," Mr. Walder said. "Come, Mrs. Walder will show you inside and take you to your room where you can unpack. Then we'll sit down for dinner together."

At dinner, Alfons politely explained to the Walders that he was vegetarian and would gladly eat the dairy, grain and vegetable offerings, but would not eat any of the meat or chicken that was served. This was his way of creating the expectations up front for his desire to keep a kosher diet as best as possible.

"How about fish?" Mrs. Walder inquired. "Will you eat fish as a source of protein?"

## Chapter 30

"Yes, certainly," Alfons answered, "but no lobsters or crabs. Those have never sat well in my stomach." Alfons did not get into the details that ocean bottom crawlers were not considered kosher.

"Alfons, we'll be sure to cook plenty of salmon and tuna for you," Mrs. Walder seemed willing to accommodate Alfons' diet and didn't second guess his requests.

"Alfons, I want you to get a good night's sleep. We're going to wake you early to take you through your responsibilities on the farm," Mr. Walder informed him.

"What will my schedule be like?" Alfons asked.

"Well, for starters, you'll need to wake early," Mr. Walder began. "At four o'clock in the morning, you'll begin to milk the cows in the barn. We use the milk for our family and for baking breads and cakes in the bakery. You'll dress for school and at six o'clock we'll take the horse into the village where we will deliver the breads and baked goods to groceries and cafes."

Alfons nodded his head in understanding.

"Once we've finished our routes, I'll drop you off at the high school. The walk from school is about three kilometers back to the farm. When you return home, you will work in the fields and help wrap the baked goods in preparation for the next day's delivery. We'll have dinner as a family and then you can retire back to your bedroom to finish your school work and prepare for bed."

At this point, Alfons was beginning to worry that this arrangement was too arduous for him. Like all the challenges he faced up until this point, he would find a way to make it work. He didn't need much, just the serenity knowing that he would not need to run or hide from relentless enemies.

## Live and Be Counted

"I'm looking forward to the busy schedule," Alfons responded dutifully, "and grateful to have a home here."

The routine turned out to be difficult for Alfons, especially on cold winter mornings when it was preferable to remain tucked in bed. During the spring season, Alfons was busy on the farm planting seeds and drawing irrigation lines. During the fall season he helped with the harvest, bringing stalks of wheat into the bakery's storage units and assortments of grown vegetables into the house. He joined Mr. Walder on the delivery routes each morning to the groceries and cafes.

Alfons took his studies seriously at the high school and earned respectable marks in math, history and science, despite so much interruption in his schooling over the prior five years. Each day, he wrapped his forehead and arm with his *t'fillin*, just as he did while he was in the monastery and every day since his *Bar Mitzvah*.

As his father had promised, Alfons traveled back to the Morgins refugee camp three times a year for Jewish holidays to celebrate Rosh Hashanah, Passover and Chanukah with his parents and sister. When he visited the camp, he picked up the responsibilities he had carried before his adoption into the foster family. He was counted on to haul twenty-five liters of milk across his shoulders from the farm eight kilometers away. He helped bake Passover *matzahs* in the kitchen, the flat bread which served as the dining centerpiece of the Passover holiday. He led songs and told stories from the Bible to the children in their classrooms.

While he was in Pfaeffikon, the Walder's fulfilled their commitment to Alfons by including him as a member of the family. He grew fond of the older Walder children who were closest in age to him and reciprocated the appreciation with hard work on the family's farm and bakery. He continued to progress in school as if he had never missed a day.

## Chapter 30

The Swiss social worker assigned to the foster children near Zurich visited Alfons every few months to check in on his welfare. "I love the Walder family, they have treated me kindly since the moment I arrived," Alfons exclaimed. "But I miss celebrating the *Shabbat* and attending synagogue. Maybe there is a Jewish family in Zurich with whom I can spend the weekends during the summer once the school year has concluded. I'm sure the Walders would appreciate time for themselves without me, just as well."

The social worker located a Jewish family in the city of Zurich that was religiously observant like Alfons. He looked forward to spending *Shabbat* in a familiar environment, eating the traditional foods of gefilte fish, chicken soup and cholent. On his first weekend visit, however, Alfons felt the family looking at him pitifully and he was relegated to eat in a side room with the maid apart from the family.

Jews living in the large cities of Switzerland were not directly affected by the Nazi occupation in the surrounding countries. Alfons felt that this particular family looked at him blamefully for what was happening to European Jewry. Not that he specifically was to blame, but that they felt the Jews must have done something to bring about the hatred and ire of the Germans.

Alfons' discomfort and sense of unwelcoming elevated throughout his visit. He told the social worker that he would prefer to continue living at the Walders and no longer wanted to have an alternative option for the weekend.

At nights, Mr. Walder took Alfons to the family room where they had a large radio box that stood between two rocking chairs. They listened to music, game shows and storytelling, and turned up the dial when the radio host delivered updates on the war. In 1943, England led an audacious bombing raid against dams, bridges and buildings in the industrial area of Western

## Live and Be Counted

Germany. Italy surrendered to the Allied Forces, allowing US and British forces to land in southern Italy and force the Germans back up the Italian peninsula. In 1944, Allied forces with Canadian soldiers successfully landed on the beaches of Normandy in France, opening a second and critical ground battle against the Germans. The Allied Forces pushed their way into France and successfully regained control of Paris within a few months.

At the beginning of 1945, the Germans attempted a final counter-offensive to push back the Allied Forces in Belgium and cut off the supply port in Antwerp. The battle lasted almost six weeks during the harsh winter and left massive casualties on both sides. In the spring of 1945, the Allied Forces, led by the United States, continued to advance into Germany and persevered in closing in on the western side of Berlin. With the Russians advancing from the eastern side, the German capital was fully surrounded.

On April 30, 1945, the British Broadcasting Company delivered the announcement that both shocked Alfons and brought happy tears streaming down his face. Adolf Hitler had committed suicide by a single gunshot to the head. The man who singularly ripped apart Alfons' childhood and brought an entire continent to ruins was dead. One week later on May 7, Germany unconditionally surrendered to the western Allied Forces.

The damage, however, had already been done. News of the atrocities committed by the Nazis was reported daily by the BBC radio broadcast over the following weeks. More than twenty concentration camps enslaving Jews across Germany, Austria and Poland had been discovered. Jewish communities throughout Europe had been eradicated and millions of lives were extinguished. Many Jewish prisoners were liberated from the concentration camps, however most of them, now orphaned or widowed, suffered from starvation, gangrene, scabies, typhus and tuberculosis among other illnesses.

## Chapter 30

Almost all of those who were freed had nowhere to go.

On May 17, the two-day Jewish festival of *Shavuot* venerating God's giving of the Ten Commandments to Moses on Mount Sinai, commenced. Alfons was unable to travel back to Morgins to be with his family, but he also did not want to work on those days and desecrate the sanctity of the holiday.

He approached his foster father and said, "Mr. Walder, the Jewish people of Europe have suffered catastrophic losses. Losses no human could ever fathom. Our leaders have called upon Jewish survivors to observe a two-day fast to commemorate the millions of our people who perished during the war and to pray for healing and rebuilding. With your permission, I will fast for two days along with my people and not go to school or perform work on the farm."

In reality, the leadership of European Jewry had been decimated and there was no such effort to organize a widespread fast in response to the Nazi atrocities. Fasting for two days was a zealous undertaking, but his faith in God grew firmer and more secure over the past five years. The war was over and the three people who mattered most to him were alive and well.

They had made it through, sometimes apart from each other, sometimes together.

During the war, while he was in hiding and on the run, it wasn't always possible for Alfons to observe the Jewish holidays. Living in Toulouse, the holidays were not the same without his father. While he was hidden in the monastery, he lost track of the Hebrew calendar.

For two days, Alfons fasted alone for the millions of Jews who would never sit around a *Shabbat* table again. He fasted for the thousands of orphaned children who would never see their parents again. He fasted for the countless number of parents bearing the excruciating pain of having their children stripped from their arms and sent to their deaths.

Alfons himself felt fortunate and blessed. His family would rebuild their lives. They would once again celebrate *Shabbat* and the Jewish festivals together. He would live to see his parents grow old together. He would continue to be a big brother to Helgi.

Alfons waited until he finished school in May to say goodbye to the Walders and return to his family in Morgins. There was a lot for which to be forlorn, but there was also a lot for which to be grateful.

"Gather around now!" Elsa called to all the children in the courtyard at recess at the end of May. "Helgi's father is going to take a picture to remember our school year."

Elsa was excited to celebrate the end of the war, but there was still much she did not know. Was it really safe for them outside of the refugee camp? Where would she and her family go from here? What would happen to the orphaned children that lived with them at Morgins? What became the fate of hers and Alexander's families from Vienna?

Thirty-six Jewish children scattered around the benches in the courtyard. All of them displaced and chased from their homes over the past four years. Most, like Alfons and Helgi, also had to scale mountains, cross rivers and brave dangerous terrain to make it into Switzerland. All of them originated from Germany, Austria or France. Some had parents with them while others had become orphans during the war or separated from their parents whose fate remained unknown, smuggled across the border by members of the French Resistance.

"Smaller children sit down on the ground or on the bench in front. Taller children and teenagers stand in the back!" Elsa instructed them.

## Chapter 30

Together, they had made the best of difficult conditions and created a temporary community that kept them from the reach of the Nazis during the later years of the war. It was far from perfect, but they had all been motivated to recreate a sense of normalcy with whatever means they had.

Alfons, eighteen years old at this time, took his place in the back row behind the smaller children on the bench in front of him, his elbows pointing outward in right angles as he locked his hands against his hips.

"Everyone say cheese!" Alexander cried out as he framed the group through his Kodak Vigilant Junior Six-20 folding camera that he bought in Evian near Lake Geneva. He adjusted the focus dial a few nodes until he was satisfied with the sharpness of the image and pushed the button.

"Swiss cheese!" thirty-six cheery faces roared back in unison and then, as if it were rehearsed, erupted in Jewish songs of peace and thanksgiving, connecting their hands to form a large dancing circle.

Alfons, his parents and all the adults that were with them outside for the picture followed the lead of the younger children, forming their own dancing circle.

There was still a lot unknown, but they had made it through.

# Chapter 31

July 30, 2020

In the middle of the summer, COVID-19 was still a serious threat. The warm weather helped bring people outside where aerosols were more likely to dissipate than to infect. However, it gave many a false sense of security that morphed small gatherings into larger ones, weakening vigilance that was needed to prevent the spread of the deadliest virus in the last one hundred years. There was also a growing lethargy around general restrictions and mask wearing, leading to activities and behaviors more reminiscent before the pandemic, rather than those needed to help curb infection rates.

Eli and his friends also knew that the calendar flipping into August would bring the conversation back to school, which was frantically preparing to reopen in September. Some schools reimagined ways to create safe, in-person learning. Eli's school was one of them.

Parents, teachers, and admittedly most of the children, wanted to be back at school and not have to take classes on Zoom from their bedrooms or kitchens. Teachers and students muscled through March, April, May and June through distant learning because there was no other choice. However, there were fears that continuing in an all-virtual learning environment could widen an educational divide between those students capable and equipped to learn through Zoom and those who were not. Schools formed taskforces made up of medical experts and other contributors who were establishing protocols needed to operate the schools safely.

## Chapter 31

Throughout the summer, Eli maintained occasional Zoom sessions with his grandfather.

"We listened to the principal explain all of the new rules that were put in place in order to reopen the school," Eli described to Papa. "Everyone will need to wear masks, desks will be socially distanced and we'll need to quarantine if anyone in our classroom or on our bus route gets COVID-19."

Alfons was skeptical if the schools would be successful in preventing the spread of the virus. He worried that without a vaccine or clear treatment, community transmission could be tragic.

"Children can get sick and also be potential carriers of the virus, transmitting it to someone who could become seriously ill," Papa said thoughtfully.

"It sure will be good when a vaccine is ready, then everything will go back to normal," Eli commented. "Like when World War Two ended and everyone was able to return to their homes."

Alfons knew that it took many years before people considered their life back to some normalcy after World War Two ended. Europe was left in ruins, with ubiquitous starvation, illness and homelessness. Life certainly did not return to the way it was. "Eli, Jews were not welcomed back to their homes, and those that tried to go back found their villages desolate, their synagogues wrecked and their schools in heaps of rubble."

Alfons took a moment to reflect on the vast devastation that had taken place. Whole communities, thriving schools and entire families were extinguished, not by an atomic bomb, but by a sinister plan that resulted in the systemic deaths of six million men, women and children.

## Live and Be Counted

"Some tried hopelessly to find relatives lost during the war," Papa continued. "Others lived in displaced persons camps for several years while seeking visas to the United States, Israel, England, Australia or anywhere that would accept them. It took years for Holocaust survivors to rebuild a fraction of what had been violently and unjustly taken from them."

"I didn't think about that, but you're right," Eli confessed. "Think about all the people who recently lost jobs or their businesses when the government ordered the lockdowns. Think about the children who lost their parents or siblings to the virus. It could take years for people to rebuild their lives."

Eli thought for a moment. His great grandfather had told him stories of remarkable faith and survival, but there were also enormous losses. "Papa, what happened to all of your aunts, uncles and cousins who used to live near you in Vienna."

"All of my family remained behind in Vienna after we fled to Paris and we presumed they were all murdered or sent to the gas chambers. We never when back to Vienna, afraid that we would be blamed for the destruction."

Eli stared back at Papa with an enormous sense of loss, never returning to Vienna to look for their family or claiming back their apartment that they were forced to abandon.

"Papa, now that the war was over, did you come to America?" Eli's immigration project had been submitted several months before, capturing as much as he could to describe Papa's travails through Europe and ultimately submitting a shortened version for his teacher.

"After Germany's surrender in May 1945, I stayed with the Walders for another six weeks to finish school and became a high school graduate!"

## Chapter 31

"Congratulations, Papa!"

"Considering how many schools I had attended since I was eleven, you would have thought I was a problem child with deplorable behavior!" Papa laughed.

Papa related how three months after the war ended refugees in Morgins were permitted to return to France and settled in a small city in eastern France near the border with Switzerland.

"My parents and sister lived in Aix-les-Bains, but I wanted to continue my education and applied to Sorbonne University in Paris, where I was accepted to start in September of 1946."

"Isn't college really expensive? How did you afford tuition?" Eli asked.

"Sorbonne was a public university and the admissions department allowed me to attend for free. The French government felt that bringing students back to university was an investment in the rebuilding process for the country. I studied liberal arts and took a part-time job with a furrier called Wein & Co. in Paris assembling mink coats. During the winter and summer breaks, I went to the city of Nice in the south of France to sell coats to Arabian and Asian nobility that vacationed on the Balearic Sea."

"Papa, it sounds like you had the perfect experience having worked in the coat store in Vienna," Eli said.

"I was grateful to have a job, and I was pretty good at it too. I even remember the process of cleaning and cutting the mink furs and sewing them into coats," Papa recollected.

"On the side, I also bought cigarettes from American soldiers stationed in Paris", Papa continued. "Thousands of soldiers remained in Europe after the war to resettle displaced persons and help rebuild the government and infrastructure. The American soldiers loved cigarettes, but they had more than they could use. Back then, no one knew about their harmful effects. I bought the excess cartons from them and resold the cigarettes to the staff and guests at French hotels across the city."

"One evening, I accidently walked into a police station to sell cigarettes thinking it was a hotel! I got out of there very quickly!" Papa mused. "After paying for my living expenses, I sent all the money I earned back to my parents in Aix-les-Bains. I continued going to university and working part-time at the furrier for two years. Almost every weekend, I traveled nine hours by train to spend *Shabbat* with my parents."

"It doesn't sound like life became any easier for you," Eli could feel once again the responsibility Papa had for his family.

"Life was hard. We pulled francs together to make ends meet, but it was far from the life we had in Vienna. Father tried to back into the coat business, but he never really gained momentum. The war had taken a toll on him and he took low paying jobs whenever there was work available."

Alfons explained how many Jewish survivors sought entry to the United States. "The United States was built by immigrants and served as a beacon of freedom to the entire world. One weekend during the summer of 1948, we received a specially marked envelope with the seal of the United States. Mother scurried carefully to open it up and elatedly pulled out our newly granted visas to America.

"Papa, why did it take so long for the visas to arrive if the war had ended in 1945?" Eli asked.

"At the end of the war, European Jews were not allowed to resettle in the US. The United States largely kept its borders closed in the years following the war. The government did not

## Chapter 31

want to be responsible for housing and feeding thousands of refugees who had nowhere to go. Its primary concern was resettling the millions of soldiers that were deployed around the world during the war and returning the country to its normal way of life. Eventually, the US changed its immigration policies after growing political pressure and the moral obligation it has always felt to provide haven to persecuted peoples. In 1948, the US began to issue visas to Holocaust survivors who remained displaced, provided they had a sponsor."

"What exactly is a sponsor?" Eli asked.

"A sponsor is someone who promises to help you when you first arrive to the United States. Someone who can find you housing and a job, and possibly give you money to help get you started so you don't become dependent on the government."

"Who sponsored you to come? You never mentioned having any relatives in the US," Eli speculated.

"My father had a business partner in New York. His name was William Lapoten, the same balding man in the tweed sports jacket that I met when I was ten years old and joined my father on a business trip to Paris in 1937. This was the man who asked us how the Jews in Vienna were feeling about Adolf Hitler's rise to power in Germany, which was the first time I had ever heard Hitler's name. William Lapoten became our American sponsor."

"The next month in September 1948, we took a train to the port city of Cannes in the southeast of France and boarded the MS Sobieski to sail across the Atlantic. The MS Sobieski was a Polish passenger ship that had been used to transport Allied soldiers from Northern Africa to France. We voyaged on the seas for ten days until we reached the oh-so admired Statue of Liberty in the New York harbor."

## Live and Be Counted

"Papa, tell me more about what the boat ride was like," Eli said curiously, thinking this would give him additional details on Papa's actual journey to America.

"We had very tight sleeping quarters and ate in a large dining hall. For the first few days, we were all nauseous from the rocking waves of the sea, but eventually we felt better. There were other Jewish families on their way to New York with visas just like us. Our boat departed at the end of September 1948, just after the High Holidays of *Rosh Hashanah* and *Yom Kippur*."

"That means you must have been on the boat for the holiday of *Succot*," Eli said, referring to the festival when Jews commemorate the protection that God afforded them in the desert after the Exodus from Egypt by living in temporarily huts outside their homes.

"It's funny you should mention that," Papa smiled at a fond memory. "While we were on the ship, several teens and young adults I befriended built a small *succah* on the top deck from canvas and poles we found on the ship. Each of the families took turns eating one of the meals in the *succah* to celebrate the holiday."

"It was probably the first time that anyone ever ate in a *succah* on the Atlantic Ocean!" Eli was excited by the prospect.

"After a ten-day journey, we arrived in New York and met William Lapoten who had already put a security deposit on a small apartment for us in Brooklyn. He helped my parents start a dry goods store at the corner that became their livelihood for the next thirty years. The store never reached the same levels of success as our store in Vienna, but it was enough to sustain our family."

Alfons reminded himself that he also worked in a store that sold draperies and tablecloths to help supplement the family's income, and from there he went on to sell household appliances.

## Chapter 31

Unfortunately, he never had the opportunity to finish college after arriving in America. The two years he spent studying at Sorbonne University in Paris was as far as he was able to go.

"Eli, let me tell you something extraordinary. When we first arrived in New York, William Lapoten presented me with a picture of a man sitting in a chair holding a baby and told me that he was the man in the picture and that I was the baby!"

"How did he have a picture of you?" Eli wondered.

"It turns out, he had travelled to Vienna in 1927 to meet with Father a few months after I was born. Father took a picture with William's camera as he was holding me in a chair. William had the photo developed and held onto the picture for more than twenty years until he met us again in New York."

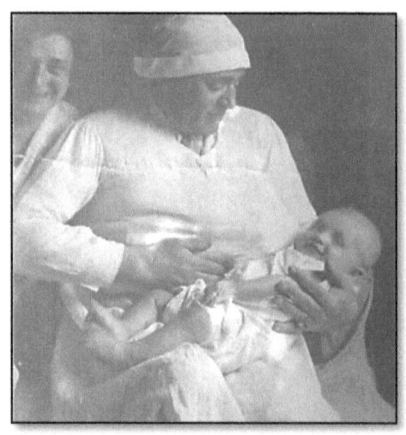

"Papa," Eli's voice dipped morosely. "You don't have any pictures from your childhood, do you?"

"Very few," Papa answered dejectedly. "We left almost everything behind in Vienna. The only articles we took with us were my mother's gold jewelry and the *t'fillin* I got for my *Bar Mitzvah*. I have the baby picture from William Lapoten and the picture with my mother where I'm holding my sister after she was born, both of which I dearly treasure. There's also the small photo from my false identification papers from the French underground. Other than that, I really have no pictures from the first eighteen years of my life."

## Live and Be Counted

"Papa, did you ever go back to Vienna to see where you grew up?"

Alfons thought pensively how they left everything behind. "Even though Hitler was dead, Nazi soldiers and sympathizers still lived throughout the former German Empire. We never went back or heard from anyone from the family who lived in Vienna. We presumed they had all been murdered."

"Papa, I'm so sorry to hear that." A lump formed in Eli's throat.

"Thank you, Eli," Papa acknowledged his compassion. "Many years later in 2012 I went back to Vienna for the first time. Without any warning, I received a peculiar letter in a calligraphy-addressed envelope with special postmarks. It was an invitation from President Heinz Fischer of Austria requesting my presence on behalf of the Austrian government."

"What did he want from you? What could you possibly have done wrong?"

"Oh no, nothing that I did wrong!" Papa laughed ironically. "The President decided after all these years to apologize to Austrian Jews who were expelled or forced to run. An olive branch, if you will, to forge a reconciliation with Jewish Holocaust survivors and their children."

"Papa, why would anyone want to go back? They killed your family and took your home."

"I didn't want to go," Papa confessed. "Grandma Phyllis encouraged me to accept the invitation as a way of bringing closure to a childhood that was abruptly cut short. She said convincingly that the leadership of today is not necessarily the leadership of yesterday. There were Austrian Jews that survived the camps and did return to Vienna. Today, there are fewer than

## Chapter 31

fifteen thousand Jews living in Vienna compared to two-hundred and fifty thousand before the war. Our visit would strengthen their resolve and let them know that they were not alone in the fight against anti-Semitism."

"That sounds like a good argument. Did you decide to go in the end?"

"Yes, we did. Holocaust survivors went anywhere they could since visas were scarce in the years following the end of World War Two. We were joined by about two hundred former Austrian Jews who had settled in Israel, England, Australia, South Africa, Uruguay, Mexico, Argentina, and of course the US. The Austrian government wined and dined us with kosher food and we spent *Shabbat* at the Seitenstettengasse Temple, which was the only synagogue in the city to remain standing after Kristallnacht."

Alfons remembered how President Fischer was conciliatory and offered financial incentives if the survivors would consider moving back to Austria. "I believed his motives were in earnest, a true act of reconciliation, but there was no way any of us were accepting the offer."

"I walked past the apartment building where we lived, but I had no desire to go upstairs and knock on the door. There were pleasant memories growing up in that apartment, our *Shabbat* meals, my mother making chicken soup, my father playing the piano, singing songs with my aunts, uncles and cousins around the table, playing games with Ludwig. It was best to keep those moments preserved in my mind and not distort them with new images of the inside."

"Papa, there were many people who helped you make it through the Holocaust." Hearing Papa's story conclude so many years later back with an invitation to return to Austria made Eli rerun all the events and people who played a critical role in Papa's survival.

Eli remembered Josef Lowenherz in Vienna, and Helena Bensimon in Paris. There was the farmer who let them sleep in the barn on the way to Bordeaux and Monsieur Martin who extended them an apartment in Toulouse. There was Alice who brought Papa to the monastery and the Abbott who taught you while you were hidden. Mr. Chezmann from the cheese farm and the Walders who was Papa's foster family in Switzerland. And, of course, Mr. Lapoten who was responsible for bringing them to the United States.

Papa was impressed how much of the story Eli replayed. As he heard him list all the names, it occurred to Papa that most of the people who were responsible for helping to save his family weren't even Jewish. They were simple men and women who put their own lives at risk to hide or usher friends, neighbors and strangers to safety. They had a choice to ignore what was happening to their Jewish neighbors, but they didn't.

"Papa, your story has heroes and that's why you survived the Holocaust."

"It's what you do and the impact you have on other that counts in people's lives the most," Papa said, but he also knew that six million Jews did not have anyone who helped them, and their stories would never be told.

"God continued to bless us with a new opportunity and long life in America. My mother and father died peacefully in their mid-eighties and were proud of each one of their seven grandchildren. Today, there are more than twenty great grandchildren through me and my sister. Each one of those descendants represents a small tribute to the one and a half million

## Chapter 31

children, amongst the six million Jews, who perished during the Holocaust."

Eli listened in silence. He didn't have to say anything to appreciate the enormity of the moment and his role in honoring the traditions and observances that continued through his great-great grandparents. He suddenly felt this intrinsic connection to Papa's father, but realized it wasn't so sudden at all. The connection to Papa's father had been growing since he first learned about his wit and heroism at the start of the pandemic.

"You know Eli, when you were born your parents named you in memory of my father," Papa informed him. "His name was Alexander and when your names are spelled in Hebrew, you both share the first two letters *Alef* and *Lamid*."

"I knew that I was named after Grandpa Alexander," Eli admitted. "I did not really know who he was or anything about his life. Now I know, and I couldn't be any prouder to be named for such a strong, faithful Jew."

"There's something else I want to tell you," Papa continued. "My father didn't share much about his time during the war. He kept his experiences private, especially the time he was interned in Gurs and Rivesaltes. Do you remember how he helped contrive an escape plan in Rivesaltes for a German Jewish couple?"

"I do! I think their names were Rose and Julius, right?"

"Right," Papa answered. "It turns out, that was not the last time that my father saw them."

"You mean they survived the war?"

"After escaping from Rivesaltes pretending to see an obstetrician doctor, Rose and Julius fled south and crossed the French border into Spain. After the war, they corresponded by mail with the Dutch family in The Hague and were relieved to hear that their daughter Clare had maintained her hiding place in the attic and avoided discovery by the Nazis. Their older son Richard, had been discovered by the Nazis and spent the war years in a labor camp in Rotterdam but he survived and reunited with Clare in The Hague. After Julius and Rose were able to confirm their exact location in letters they wrote after the war, the two teenagers took a train from The Hague to Spain and awaited visas with their parents, like we did, to immigrate to the United States."

Several years later living in New York, Clare and Alfons were set up on a date. They went out several times, but suddenly America found itself in the midst of another war, this time in Korea. They decided to become engaged to be married so that Alfons would be exempt from the military draft.

"While we were dating, Clare and I shared our childhood and survival stories from Europe, but there was no expectation that we had ever crossed paths. After we became engaged, my parents invited their parents for dinner to our apartment in Brooklyn. Helgi was twelve years old at the time and peeked curiously from the kitchen when the door buzzer rang."

As soon as they walked through the door, Alexander looked shockingly at Clare's parents and cried out, *'Julius! Is it you? Is it really you?'*

"I still get chills today when I think about Julius weeping uncontrollably as he embraced my father and said *'It is me, Alexander. Yes, it is really me.'*"

# Chapter 32

### August 2020

Eli submitted his immigration assignment long before his great grandfather finished telling him the story about how he came to America. He wrote the short version that consisted of being born in Austria, hiding from the Nazis during World War Two, and immigrating to New York on a large passenger ship in 1948. When asked to relate his great grandfather's favorite food while growing up, Eli described the Passover *matzahs* that Alfons had baked with his own father for the five hundred people who were living together in the Morgins refugee camp in Switzerland.

The summer was concluding and Eli's school had received approval from the governor to open, albeit with classroom modifications that would create as much social distancing as possible. There was a bible worth of other rules to determine when a child would be required to quarantine at home if they were exposed to someone who was suspected of having or tested positive for COVID-19.

Just before school was ready to resume, Eli sent Papa an email requesting an impromptu Zoom session. "Papa, remember when you told me about how your family lived at the Morgins refugee camp in Switzerland?" Eli asked.

Papa didn't need the reminder. Morgins had become a haven in Switzerland during the latter part of the war for Jews who were fortunate to have escaped from Nazi occupied lands.

Eli continued, "I did a Google search the other day for *Morgins Refugee Camp* and a few results appeared. The first hit

## Live and Be Counted

that appeared stated '*Children in the Morgins refugee camp school pose with their teacher by a fence*'. So, I clicked on the link and a black and white photograph appeared that looked to be from the olden days. The quality of the picture was actually very good, not grainy as I would have expected. I wondered if you knew anybody from the photo?"

"Eli, can you share your screen? Let me see if I recognize anyone in the photo," Papa said skeptically.

Eli clicked on the *Share Screen* icon at the bottom of his Zoom frame and navigated to the open browser that contained the photo. The web page loaded from top to bottom, and as it did, Alfons' heart began to beat a little harder in anticipation.

Initially a large group of young, smiling children posing for a camera captured his attention. At first glance, it hardly seemed to be a photo with anyone he would possibly recognize.

Then Alfons saw it and is heart raced even faster. He jumped up from his seat and took a few steps back in disbelief.

"Phyllis!" he shouted to her from the top of the stairs. "Phyllis, you have to come up here. You have to see this!"

Alfons sat back down in front of the screen and stared skeptically back at the photo. He blinked his eyes several times, trying to clear them of the tears beginning to form.

There was no doubt what he was seeing.

Staring back at him from the top row on the right was an unmistakably a younger version of himself. A tall, well-groomed seventeen-year-old Alfons, his elbows pointing outward with his hands locked against his hips. He was captured in a group photo with the Morgins children from seventy-seven years ago. A picture

## Chapter 32

he never knew existed, a picture he suddenly remembered being taken.

Eli watched his great grandfather look shockingly at the photograph and saw tears swell in his eyes. "Papa, are you OK?"

Phyllis hurried upstairs, nervous that she was being summoned for help. She Alfons seated safely at the desk and leaned across the back of his shoulder to look at the photograph on the screen.

"Alfons!" Phyllis cried pointing at the top right of the photo. "That's you! That's you! Where is this picture from? Where did you find it?"

The tears continued to swell in his eyes. Papa took his fingers and tried to wipe the teardrops flowing down his cheeks. He stood up from the desk and walked out of sight from the computer screen.

"Papa, come back! Did I just hear Grandma Phyllis correctly?" Eli stammered. "You're in the picture?"

Papa circled back again to the desk and sat down in the chair, coming back into focus on his iPad. "Yes, Eli! That's me. That's me in the last row on the right, wearing a white shirt and coat," Papa exclaimed, but could barely muster the words from his weeping voice as tears continued to roll down his cheeks.

"I thought that was the teacher mentioned in the caption," Eli tried to find a way to test Papa's surety. He too was incredulous that Papa would truly be in such an old photograph he found on the Internet.

## Live and Be Counted

"That's not the teacher, that's me! I'm eighteen years old in that picture. I was always tall and grown-up looking for my age. That's why Alice had so much difficulty hiding me in the orphanage and brought me to the monastery instead where I could blend in as an adult with other monks."

Eli looked back at the photo and he also saw it. A younger, very handsome version of his great grandfather standing proudly with thirty-five other children who similarly had escaped from the grip of the Nazis.

"And there is my sister! That's Helgi!" Papa pointed to a girl in the middle of the photo who was no older than six years. I can't believe this photo exists. The only picture that I have during a ten-year span is a small passport photo. I'm looking at myself for the first time in my life as a teenager. Eli, I can't believe you found this picture!"

Eli scrolled down and a second back and white photograph of similar good quality, this one with a dozen or so adults holding random kitchen utensils and laughing joyfully at the camera.

## Chapter 32

"Hold the screen there," Papa said, the adrenaline continuing to pump hard through his heart. He lifted his finger to the iPad and rested it right in the center of the photo. Tears as large as love itself fell from his eyes.

"Mother," Papa whispered. He used his index finger and thumb to zoom in on the picture. "I had forgotten what you looked like, how beautiful you were." Elsa was standing tall on a bench in the back row, her head leaning to the right.

Alfons looked at the words posted underneath the photo and saw that it was part of the online collection published by the United States Holocaust Memorial Museum. He recalled his father taking pictures with the camera he had bought in Evian and converting a storage room at the Morgins lodge into a dark room to print the photographs. He recalled his father organizing the children for a photo and surmised that he must have done that same thing for a group of adults. He could not believe these two photos survived the war and had been sent to Holocaust Museum in Washington DC.

### Live and Be Counted

"Papa, aren't there people who deny the Holocaust ever happened? These pictures validate everything you shared with me. A photo like that is undeniable!"

Papa took a deep breath. Waves of additional memories pulsated through his body, triggered by the searing vision of the photograph in which he was pictured. He looked closely and carefully counted each of the heads. Thirty-six smiling children that evaded the Nazis attempt to extinguish Jewish life. Thirty-six Jewish souls that survived mankind's worst atrocity of genocide. Papa didn't overlook the significance of the number thirty-six.

"Two times *chai*," Papa said, referencing the numeric value of the Hebrew letters that made up the word for *life* in English.

Except for his sister Helgi, Alfons did not recognize or remember any of the faces in photo. But he knew instinctively that each one of these precious children lived to tell their stories. Like him, each one of them lived with the unimaginable burden of rebuilding after suffering through an immense loss of life around them.

Alfons knew that each one of these Jewish children lived to be counted.

# Personal Reflections

### Ronald Siesser

I have always wanted to tell my grandfather's story. When the COVID-19 pandemic mercilessly swept across the globe during the first few months of 2020, the cruel reality of my grandparents being forced to shelter in their home elevated the desire to check-in and talk with them more frequently. Zoom had quickly become a household term, and by the end of March, we had taught Papa how to join a Zoom call with his audio and video buttons on simultaneously.

In April 2020, four weeks into the lockdown and closure of schools, my daughter Atara's school, Yavneh Academy in Paramus, NJ, was preparing to commemorate *Yom HaShoah* (Holocaust Remembrance Day), but had to rethink its original plans through remote learning. With Papa becoming increasingly comfortable on Zoom, he agreed to share his story with the middle school students during a special virtual assembly. I sent the link to family members and during the presentation Papa told stories from his survival that we had never heard before.

I'm grateful to Rabbi Shmuel Burstein, Yavneh Academy's Director of Jewish History and Holocaust Studies, for preparing my grandfather and facilitating the discussion as Zoom host in an interview-like style. This appreciation extends to the administrative leadership of Yavneh Academy, including Rabbi Jonathan Knapp, Rabbi Steven Penn and Mrs. Barbara Rubin, who organized the *Yom HaShoah* program for the middle school students and helped bring Papa's story to them.

## Personal Reflections

Papa's concluding words to the Yavneh Academy students linked the pandemic crisis faced by the current generation with the trauma his generation experienced in the late 1930s and early 1940s. The situations were vastly different, but there were similarities in which the students could relate to going into hiding, abandoning schools and deserting synagogues. The students and faculty of Yavneh Academy were deeply moved how Papa maintained his faith in God throughout the war, and he encouraged the students to do the same as they fought against a modern, viral enemy.

About a month after the *Yom HaShoah* presentation, my younger son Eli in fifth grade had an immigration project that required him to interview someone who was born outside the United States and came to this country. Naturally, he interviewed my grandfather over Zoom and included the recipe for Passover *matzahs* in an Immigrant Cookbook that his class assembled. Papa and his father baked the *matzahs* for the 483 Jews residing at the Morgins refugee camp in Switzerland between 1942 and 1945.

Using the *Yom HaShoah* presentation as the outline, and applying the unfolding crisis of the COVID-19 pandemic as a backdrop, I began to write my grandfather's story. In reality, it was me talking to him most days and Eli joined when he could. I felt that telling the story through the eyes of a boy living through a pandemic who was the same age as Papa at the start of World War Two provided a meaningful parallel.

Papa and I talked often, asking him to recount details of his youth before, during and after the war. The more we talked, the more he remembered. The more he remembered, the more I wrote.

The events and characters depicted in *Live and Be Counted* all follow the true life of Alfons Sperber and his family

## Live and Be Counted

over ten years between 1938 and 1948. I utilized a degree of creative license to construct dialogues between the figures that were part of Alfons' life during that time. The discovery of the photographs from the Morgins refugee camp which conclude *Live and Be Counted* actually occurred, although the discovery was made by me late at night while everyone was sleeping. My excitement and disbelief were audible and woke everyone up.

I can't explain why this discovery brought streaming tears of joy from my eyes. Perhaps it was the excitement to show him what I found. Perhaps it was the validation against Holocaust deniers that his experiences were real. Perhaps it was seeing the Jewish pride, despite horrifying circumstances, that emanated from the tall, strong, confident teenager.

I'm grateful to my wife Debra for encouraging me to pull out my laptop and write way into the night after the workday was done and the kids were asleep. I wasn't striving for perfection in writing this, but appreciate her role as editor and proofreader.

Thank you to my children David and Atara who allowed me to talk incessantly about the progress of the book every *Shabbat* during the lockdown periods and the months after. Our discussions about the coronavirus and newsworthy events of 2020 inspired different aspects and themes within the story.

Thank you to my youngest child Eli who allowed me to cast him as a critical part to the storytelling. A voracious reader, he provided valuable feedback on the story's themes, character development and grammar mistakes. Being the same age as my grandfather when the war broke out, Eli's perspective in living through the global pandemic made relatable experiences to the threats each one faced.

Thank you to the countless family members who allowed me to share ideas about the book and who themselves recounted

## Personal Reflections

stories that Papa had told them years before. Grandma Phyllis, who accompanied Papa on several heritage trips back to Europe, triggered memories and events that even Papa had stored away. Appreciation is extended to my Aunt Helgi, Papa's sister, and Grandma Phyllis, my mother Susan, father Steven, children David, Atara and Eli, brothers Daniel and Seth, sisters Elana and Shana, Uncle Julien, Aunt Orit and cousins Josh, Miriam Yoni and Mikey who were all important editors and contributors in helping to shape Papa's character from their own recollections of his accounts.

The fact that Alexander crafted the plan enabling Julius and Rose Teig's escape from the labor camp to Spain, which later led to the marriage of their daughter Clare to Alexander's son Alfons, can only be explained as divine intervention. Alfons and Clare were married for thirty-eight years before she passed away in 1988 from lung cancer. Though she never smoked a cigarette in her life, her doctors suspected the poor air quality living in an attic for four years in Holland permanently damaged her lungs. Alfons married Phyllis Black, one of Clare's best friends and neighbors, in 1997 after her husband Peter passed away a few years earlier.

It would also be learned that Alexander Sperber continued tuning pianos upon arriving in America, including the baby grand of his grandson Julien's future wife Orit when she learned to play as a teenager.

My final words of appreciation go to my co-author, my grandfather and my friend, Alfons Sperber. Whenever I finished writing a group of chapters, I sent them by email to Papa for review. He helped fill in the gaps, related additional experiences and corrected aspects that I got wrong. The opportunity to write a book with my grandfather may never have occurred if not for the global pandemic.

### Live and Be Counted

COVID-19 undoubtedly brought pain and suffering to thousands of people. I, myself, contracted the virus in March 2020, and fortunately overcame moderate symptoms after about two weeks of quarantining in my bedroom. In its silver lining, COVID-19 forced the world to slow down for a few moments and allowed people caught up in their daily routines to pursue interests or discover aspects of life that were always there, just waiting to be found.

It is my hope that readers will be uplifted by Alfons Sperber's courage, strength and faith during the darkest period of mankind. It has been a privilege beyond no other to be able to share his story of survival in this way as a tribute to his extraordinary life and a venerable history of our family.

May God continue to bless him, as his namesake, to live and be counted.


December 2020

# Photographs

Live and Be Counted

## Live and Be Counted

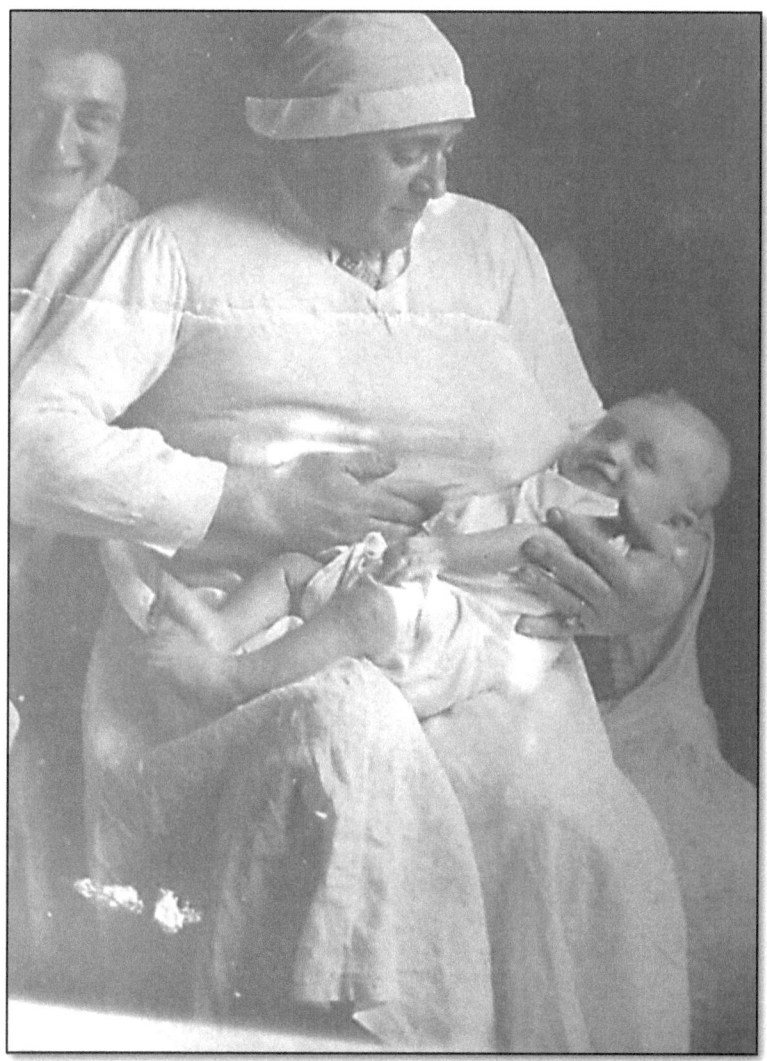

*This picture was taken by Alexander Sperber in the summer of 1927 when Alfons was just a few months old. The camera belonged to his American business partner William Lapoten who is holding Alfons and later sponsored the Sperbers' visas to the United States. Alfons' mother, Elsa Sperber, is in the back left. Alexander's business partner gave the photo to the Sperbers upon their arrival to the United States in 1948. It is the only picture Alfons has of himself as a baby.*

# Photographs

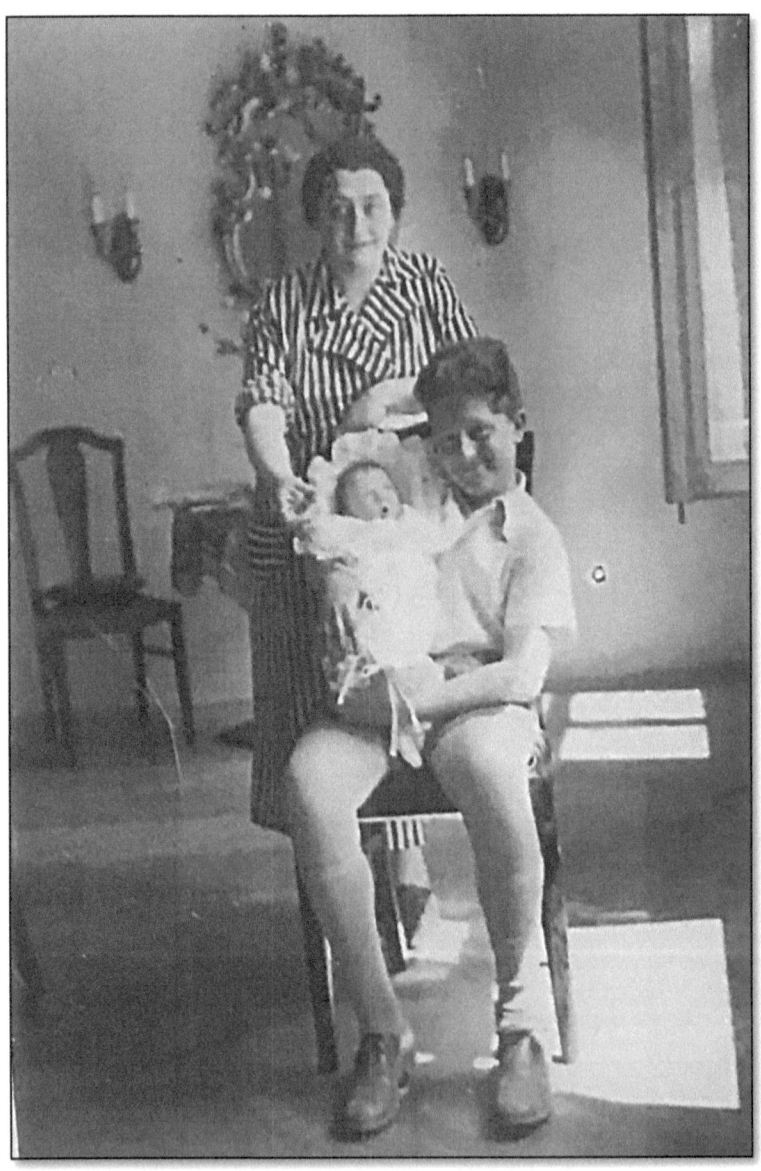

*Elsa Sperber kept this photo of her, Alfons and Helgi throughout the war. It was taken in their Vienna apartment by Alexander in 1938, soon after Helgi's birth when Alfons was eleven years old.*

## Live and Be Counted

*The St. Benedict Monastery, where Alfons was hidden as a monk for almost two years between 1941 and 1942, appears on a postcard from 1908*
.
Source: https://www.akpool.co.uk/postcards/28849541-postcard-hauute-garonne-la-trappe-de-saint-marie-vue-gnrale

Letters from Al Sperber to Alice

July 8, 1998

Dear Mrs. Synnestvedt,

It is under the most unusual circumstances I received your name from Mr. Jack Sutters of the Archives Department of the Quaker Organization in Philadelphia.

During the war in 1941, I was living with my mother near Toulouse, France when we were forced to go into hiding. I was picked up by a lady who brought me to a monastery and my little sister of 4 years to a deaf mute school. I tried to find the name and location of the monastery but so far without success. I had written to several organizations until I contacted the Quakers via Email and finally are you the lady who saved my sister's and my life?

I would love to hear from you. Maybe you can give me your telephone number.

Sincerely  Al Sperber

Al Sperber, 1998

*In 1998, Alfons located Alice Resch Synnestvedt, the woman who hid him in a monastery and Helgi in an orphanage in 1941, living in Denmark.*

*Alfons and Alice reunited in 2002 with other Holocaust survivors whom she helped save during the war. The letter Alfons wrote to Alice in 1998 was included in her memoir "Over the Highest Mountains" in 2004. A biography and picture of Alice from the 1940s appears on the American Friends Service Committee website.*

Source: https://www.afsc.org/story/alice-resch-synnestvedt-mary-elmes

## Photographs

False identifications were made for Alfons (age 15) and Helgi (age 4) in 1942 which enabled them to cross over the Alps from occupied France to neutral Switzerland with their parents.

## Live and Be Counted

*Posing with children from Morgins Refugee Camp, Alfons is standing in the back row on the right, wearing a white shirt and dark jacket. His sister Helgi is sitting in the second row, sixth from the left. In the bottom picture, Elsa Sperber is standing in the back row, second from the left, with other adults at the camp.*

*Alfons nor Helgi were aware of the photos until they were discovered by the author while writing this book. Alfons is convinced that his father took the pictures with a camera he bought while crossing into Switzerland. He made a dark room at the camp to develop the pictures and give them to families. The photos are on file at the US Holocaust Memorial Museum.*

## Photographs

*Alfons and Helgi have fun in the snow in March 1945, with Elsa Sperber smiling at the camera held by Alexander. The hotel chalet in Morgins was taken over by the Swiss government to house Jewish refugees from 1943 - 1945.*

## Live and Be Counted

*This picture was taken by Alexander Sperber in 1946 near Aix-les-Bains on a hike in the French Alps when Alfons was 19 and Helgi was 8. The Sperbers returned to France from Switzerland after the war until visas were granted to the US in 1948.*

## Photographs

*Alfons poses in the picture on the left after the war ended, taken by the Walders, who fostered him for three years in Switzerland. Mrs. Walder gave Alfons the photo when he visited her in Switzerland in 1998. On the right, Alfons is pictured in 1947 preparing a mink fur to be cut and stitched into a coat while working for a furrier Wein & Co. in Paris and attending Sorbonne University after the war.*

*Alfons' visa to the United States in 1948 depicts him as an Austrian (Osterreich) citizen. He was 21 when his family was granted permission to immigrate to New York. On the right, Alfons poses in front of the United Nations in 1949, which was located in Lake Success, NY, following a rally to admit the State of Israel to membership in the United Nations.*

## Live and Be Counted

*The MS Sobieski, a Polish passenger ship also used by Allied Forces to transport soldiers from North Africa to France during World War Two, was the ship on which Alfons Sperber and his family traveled to America in 1948.*

---

It appears that the Sperber family was immigrating to the US and not Canada. For information regarding which US institutions holds what immigration documents please se: https://www.archives.gov/research/immigration/overview

In the meantime, I located their arrival in October 1948 via New York:

Name:   Alfons Sperber
Arrival Date:   26 Oct 1948
Birth Date:   abt 1927
Age:   21
Gender:   Male
Ethnicity/ Nationality:   Austrian
Place of Origin:   Austria
Port of Departure:   Cannes, France
Port of Arrival:   New York, New York
Ship Name:   Sobieski

Traveling with parents Alexander and Elsa and sister Helga [? illeg.]

---

*An email from the Canadian Immigration Archives confirmed the Sperbers names on the passenger manifest that originated from Cannes, France and stopped in Halifax, Canada before arriving in New York.*

## Photographs

*Alfons Sperber with Clare at their wedding in 1950. His father Alexander helped Clare's parents Julius and Rose Teig escape from Rivesaltes labor camp in France and flee to Spain until the end of the war, at which point they reunited with their children Clare and Richard who were hidden in Holland.*

*The Sperbers at Helgi's wedding to Shimon Pattashnick in 1955. Alexander and Elsa Sperber are seated at the ends of the table, while Alfons and Clare stand behind them, with their three-year old daughter Susan.*

## Live and Be Counted

*Elsa and Alexander Sperber in the late 1960s standing in front of their 1962 Pontiac outside Alfons and Clare's home in Queens.*

*Julius and Rose Teig in a photo taken in the 1940s in Spain. Alexander Sperber helped the Teig's escape from Rivesaltes labor camp in 1941 in France, enabling them to flee south to Spain and reunite with their two children Richard and Clare hidden in Holland after the war. The Teig's daughter Clare met Alfons after both families immigrated to New York and married him in 1950.*

# Photographs

In 1955, Clare Sperber returned to The Hague in Holland to visit the Drielsma's, her foster family that hid her in their attic for more than four years. Clare is standing while her foster parents Tante Betty and Uncle Drill are holding Clare and Alfons' daughter Susan at three years old.

Alfons and Clare Sperber in the late 1960s

## Live and Be Counted

*Posing at Julien Sperber's Bar Mitzvah in 1970. Top Row (left to right): Shimon and Helgi Pattashnick, Elsa and Alexander Sperber, Alfons and Clare Sperber. Bottom Row (left to right): Charlotte and Richard Teig, Rose Teig.*

*The family gathers at the Sperber home in Queens in 1977 after the birth of the first great grandson to Alexander and Elsa Sperber (center on the couch), flanked by Helgi and Shimon Pattashnick. Clare Sperber, her mother Rose Teig and Julien Sperber are on the left. Susan, Steve and Ron Siesser (baby) are in the bottom row on the right. Proud grandfather Alfons Sperber was taking the picture.*

## Photographs

In 2002, Hal Myers (left) organized a reunion with about a dozen people that Alice Resch (right) helped save as children during the war. The reunion took place in South Carolina and Alice, then 94 years old flew from Denmark.

In 2012, Alfons Sperber was invited to Austria by President Heinz Fischer, along with 200 Holocaust survivors forced to flee Austria, in order to seek reconciliation. The guests were treated well, but each one declined President Fischer's offer to resettle in their country of birth. This picture was taken in front of the Sperber's apartment building where they lived in Vienna.

## Live and Be Counted

*In 1966, Alfons traveled to back to Switzerland Europe to reunite with the Walder family in Switzerland. Alfons' wife Clare and daughter Susan are in standing in the middle of the back row.*

*Alfons visited the Walders again in 1990 (top, Mr. and Mrs. Walder, with their daughter Ruth) and again in 1998 (left, with Mrs. Walder). Their son Jack Walder spent several months living with the Sperbers in the 1960s during an extended stay in New York.*

## Photographs

*Alfons presents an award in 1990 to his longtime neighbor and friend Peter Black for his leadership to the B'nai Brit organization. Peter Black, born in Berlin, was sent by his parents on a Kindertransport to the United States at age 12 in 1936 before the Holocaust. He passed away in 1994, a few years after Alfons' wife Clare died in 1988. Alfons married Peter's widow Phyllis Black in 1997.*

*Alfons and his sister Helgi at the wedding of her grandson in 2016. The two siblings have remained close their entire lives, despite eleven years of age difference.*

## Live and Be Counted

*Alfons Sperber attended a ceremony in 2011 when his grandson Ron Siesser received an award at PepsiCo, Inc. for his efforts to obtain kosher certification on the Gatorade beverage brand. His wife Phyllis Black is on the left and at right is PepsiCo's Chief Human Resources Officer Cynthia Trudell, who presented the award.*

*The Sperber, Siesser, Pattashnick and Black families celebrate Alfons Sperber's 90th birthday in March 2017.*